Investigating Emotional, Sensory and Social Learning in Early Years Practice

This book explores learning in the early years and emphasises the importance of learning in social contexts, through the senses and within close relationships. It moves away from the focus on 'learning' as the acquisition of knowledge, and instead emphasises the importance of personal, social and emotional development in early years education. The authors illustrate that young children learn best when they are supported by reliable, engaged and attentive people who know them well. This book challenges readers to reflect on their own practice and think about how emotions play a part in young children's learning and development.

Each chapter of this book discusses a different aspect of emotional, sensory and social learning, from philosophical perspectives on learning, leadership and inclusive practice, to the importance of promoting the development of children's emotional intelligence, forming close attachments to children, and encouraging them to learn through their senses. The reader is provided with a wealth of ideas and examples for application in the classroom.

Numerous practical examples, reference to contemporary research, and the authors' acknowledgement of the challenges faced by practitioners make this an inspiring and pertinent resource for new and experienced teachers and practitioners, as well as trainees and students in the fields of early years and primary education. Readers will develop the skills needed to engage in outstanding, learning-focused practice.

Sarah Cousins is Director of Early Years Programmes at the Centre for Lifelong Learning at the University of Warwick, UK. She previously led Primary and Early Years Initial Teacher Training courses at the University of Bedfordshire and London Metropolitan University, UK. Sarah is an experienced early years teacher, leader and consultant.

Wendy Cunnah is a retired academic and a grandmother. Wendy formerly acted as Head of Teacher Education and Principal Lecturer in Education at the University of Bedfordshire, UK. She led the Education Studies Programme at Sheffield Hallam University and the Master's degree programme in Inclusive Education and Dyslexia at Swansea University, UK. Wendy is an experienced education studies lecturer,

Investigating Emotional, Sensory and Social Learning in Early Years Practice

Sarah Cousins and Wendy Cunnah

Routledge
Taylor & Francis Group

LONDON AND NEW YORK

First published 2018
by Routledge
2 Park Square, Milton Park, Abingdon, Oxon OX14 4RN

and by Routledge
711 Third Avenue, New York, NY 10017

Routledge is an imprint of the Taylor & Francis Group, an informa business

British Library Cataloguing-in-Publication Data
A catalogue record for this book is available from the British Library

Library of Congress Cataloging-in-Publication Data
Names: Cousins, Sarah B., author. | Cunnah, Wendy, author.
Title: Investigating emotional, sensory and social learning in early years practice / Sarah B Cousins, Wendy Cunnah.
Description: Abingdon, Oxon ; New York, NY : Routledge, 2017.
Identifiers: LCCN 2017024679| ISBN 9781138649316 (hardback : alk. paper) | ISBN 9781138649354 (pbk. : alk. paper) | ISBN 9781315625881 (ebook)
Subjects: LCSH: Early childhood education. | Learning, Psychology of. | Perceptual learning. | Social learning. | Emotions in children. | Senses and sensation.
Classification: LCC LB1139.23 .C68 2017 | DDC 372.21--dc23
LC record available at https://lccn.loc.gov/2017024679

ISBN: 978-1-138-64931-6 (hbk)
ISBN: 978-1-138-64935-4 (pbk)
ISBN: 978-1-315-62588-1 (ebk)

Typeset in Melior
by Saxon Graphics Ltd, Derby

Printed and bound by CPI Group (UK) Ltd, Croydon, CR0 4YY

To our families and especially to Olivia Cunnah, Wendy's first grandchild.

With special thanks to Donna Stokes, Jordan Paice, Maimoonah Patel and Hannah Cunnah who shared their professional expertise with us.

Contents

Introduction

OVERVIEW OF THE CHAPTER

This chapter is about beliefs and perspectives on the topic of emotional, sensory and social learning in the early years. Love is constructed as important, and education is seen as valuable for its own sake, rather than as an investment for future economic success. Different sets of principles from international organisations are considered. The authors also put forward their own guiding principles for healthy emotional, sensory and social learning in early childhood:

- Childhood is a special time to enjoy

- Children learn about the world through their emotions, their senses and people around them

- It is important for adults to recognise and encourage children's creative expressions

- Babies and very young children thrive when they have access to the best integrated care and education

- Highly skilled and emotionally self-aware people are needed for work with babies and very young children

Introduction

A phenomenon such as learning is not possible to discuss in any straightforward manner.

(Kultti and Pramling, 2015:106)

Learning is a complex process. It is multifaceted, mysterious, and different at different times and for every child. This book considers learning in its broadest sense, particularly as it relates to young children's emotional, sensory and social learning. What does research say about learning? How do different policies in England correspond to research on the topic? What of the role of the adult? What sorts of environments support children to develop in these areas? What styles of leadership are needed?

The age-range covered in this book is broadly birth to eight, though some of the content may apply to older children. This is not to say that the chapters go through age-expectations or recommended approaches at different ages in any sequential order. Instead, there are separate chapters on different topics: theory, emotions and love, learning through the senses, learning in social contexts and leadership. Topics are covered in turn and the content in each chapter may be applied to all ages. This recursive, thematic approach accords with the authors' belief that children learn and develop in different ways and according to their own unique patterns. Things happen as they happen rather than according to pre-set plans or expectations. No child is the same, and this makes the work with young children at once fascinating and complex. As will be discussed in Chapter 2, the authors of this book are more comfortable with uncertainty than certainty, notions that draw on diverse ideas and events rather than single claims to truth. Accordingly, work with young children, families and communities is rich, unpredictable, unexpected and wonderful. Adults who choose to work with very young children have entered a highly complex field, and this explains why many admit to a vocational calling (Taggart, 2011). This book explores the intricacies of some of the work done by these highly committed people.

Children's everyday learning with family members and people who love them

Babies and young children learn from their earliest sensory and emotional experiences, through everything and everyone around them. Babies learn from expressions of love by those close to them. They see loving faces, feel loving embraces and smell the smells of the people who love them. Jean-Jacques Rousseau (1712–1778) reflected on his early learning supported by the people who surrounded him and loved him:

> How could I have learnt bad ways, when I was offered nothing but examples of mildness and surrounded by the best people in the world? It was not that the people around me – my father, my aunt, my nurse, our relatives, our friends, our neighbours – obeyed me, but rather that they loved me; and I loved them in return.
>
> (Rousseau, 2000:10)

Rousseau described a family group made up of the people who encircled him, and who guided him and cared for him with love. When young children's physical needs are met, when they can rely on their carers or educators to attend to them well, and when they feel loved, they can begin to take risks and explore their surrounding environment with confidence.

Young children's earliest emotional and sensory experiences shape their brain architecture (Murray, 2014; Lebedeva, 2015) for life and contribute to who they become as older children, and as adults. As Dowling (2010:14) articulated, 'happy memories from childhood can nourish us throughout life and we can draw on them in difficult times'.

Topics covered in different chapters of the book

This book is about creating nourishing environments that stimulate children's senses, and support them to build up a bank of positive emotional experiences. The book explores the intricate and important work of adults in early years settings, and how they contribute to children's happiness and help them to communicate well with each other.

In the introduction we consider different sets of principles. What do different organisations declare as important in early childhood? What principles underpin this book, and why are these important? In Chapter 2 we take a close look at different theories and consider how these can be applied to work with children, especially in relation to their emotional, sensory and social learning. In Chapter 3 we consider emotion and emphasise the importance of building close, loving relationships with very young children. Chapter 4 explores sensory learning, with a focus on supporting children with special educational needs and/or disabilities (SEND). Chapter 5 focuses on social learning, and how children learn in families and communities. Leadership is the topic of Chapter 6, with an emphasis on providing spaces to talk about this complex work in early childhood.

Principles and precepts

Different organisations have their own sets of guiding principles. The Early Years Regional Alliance (EYRA), run by the International Step by Step Association (ISSA), for example, is an international body made up of partners and organisations from across Europe and Central Asia. Different international stakeholders are united around a shared message and are committed to increased access, equity, quality and investment in early childhood development, education and care (ISSA, 2016). EYRA's mission is to promote a comprehensive, inclusive and rights-based approach to full development of young children and their parents. The organisation believes that this is the strongest possible foundation for the well-being of children and nations (ISSA, 2016).

Organisations such as this are engaged in important work, enabling dialogue across different professions in order to strengthen links between research, practice and policy. In order to do this important work, EYRA agreed the following principles as part of its manifesto:

- Every child has the right to a positive early childhood: realising this right is in the public interest and is the responsibility of all members of society

- The full realisation of young children's rights must be made an explicit public policy priority

- Young children thrive in nurturing, responsive, stimulating and safe family environments

- Children learn and develop through play and meaningful interactions

- All young children benefit from early childhood development services when they are inclusive and of high quality

- Building a just society for all children and their families requires proactive ways of addressing exclusion, inequality, poverty and violence

- Individualised and family-centred services support children with developmental challenges and/or disabilities to reach their full potential

- Integrated and professionalised early childhood systems support positive developmental outcomes for all young children

- Quality early childhood development services must be a priority for the allocation of public resources

(ISSA, 2016)

These are important and expansive principles. Each principle makes a particular point, but is also connected to all the other principles. So, for example, we cannot achieve the first principle, to give every child the right to a positive early childhood, if we do not also meet the third principle, and offer children a nurturing, responsive, stimulating and safe environment.

Under the principle about learning and development through play and meaningful relationships, the manifesto makes the following statement:

> Loving and respectful interactions, reading and play are essential for development and must be valued and embedded in every child's daily life: at home, in preschools and schools, in early childhood services, and the community. Families and other adults working with children should be supported to understand the importance of play and interactions with young children.

(ISSA, 2016:3)

It is encouraging that this international, interdisciplinary body of professionals makes a clear statement about the importance of loving and respectful interactions with children. Loving interactions are not restricted to familial contexts, but extended to 'other adults working with children'. There is an acknowledgement that the people who work with babies and very young children are crucially important to their healthy mental and physical development.

REFLECTION: FORMAL AND INFORMAL LEARNING

■ How are you supported to understand the importance of play and interactions with young children?

■ To what extent do you draw on your formal training?

■ To what extent do you draw on your learning from life, and intuition?

■ What is your setting policy on adult interactions with children? What, if anything, does it say about loving and respectful interactions?

Another set of principles was developed by the Center on the Developing Child at Harvard University (2016). The aim of these principles was to incorporate recent advances in the science of early childhood development and its underlying biology. The research community at the University of Harvard articulated the following principles:

1 Even infants and young children are affected adversely when significant stresses threaten their family and caregiving environments

2 Development is a highly interactive process, and life outcomes are not determined solely by genes

3 While attachments to their parents are primary, young children can also benefit significantly from relationships with other responsive caregivers both within and outside the family

4 A great deal of brain architecture is shaped during the first three years after birth, but the window of opportunity for its development does not close on a child's third birthday

5 Severe neglect appears to be at least as great a threat to health and development as physical abuse – possibly even greater

6 Young children who have been exposed to adversity or violence do not invariably develop stress-related disorders or grow up to be violent adults

7 Simply removing a child from a dangerous environment will not automatically reverse the negative impacts of that experience

8 Resilience requires relationships, not rugged individualism

The emphasis made within these principles is on quality relationships. Importantly, the principles are built on strong, interdisciplinary research. It is interesting that they convey a non-deterministic stance whereby children may or may not overcome adverse experiences, and where there is scope for positive development and recovery beyond the age of three.

REFLECTION: WINDOWS OF OPPORTUNITY FOR SENSORY, SOCIAL AND EMOTIONAL LEARNING

The following statement is made under Point 4 of the Harvard principles:

> While the regions of the brain dedicated to higher-order functions – which involve most social, emotional, and cognitive capacities, including multiple aspects of executive functioning – are … affected powerfully by early influences, they continue to develop well into adolescence and early adulthood. So, although the basic principle that 'earlier is better than later' generally applies, the window of opportunity for most domains of development remains open far beyond age 3, and we remain capable of learning ways to 'work around' earlier impacts well into the adult years.
>
> (Center on the Developing Child, 2016:2)

■ What implications does this perspective have on your practice?

As authors of this book, we too hold our own beliefs about what matters in early childhood. We have our unique perspectives. We did not write this book from a detached stance, as academics in some way cut off from the real world, with particular specialist knowledge, but as living beings, 'intertwined' (Martin and Kamberelis, 2013:672) with the world. We wrote this with our own broad experiences of living in families and working in early years contexts. We are fully involved in the world. Our learning and experiences, therefore, inevitably contributed to our writing. In other words, our informal life stories, as well as our scholarly learning and experiences as professionals, have contributed to our beliefs, and these flow into our constructions on the topic. There is no objectivity in what we write. On the contrary, our subjective stances permeate the contents of this book.

Through our accumulated knowledge and understanding about what is best for babies and young children, we agree on the following principles, and these underpin the chapters that follow:

■ Childhood is a special time to enjoy

■ Children learn about the world through their emotions, their senses and the people around them

- It is important for adults to recognise and encourage children's creative expressions

- Babies and very young children thrive when they have access to the best integrated care and education

- Highly skilled and emotionally self-aware people are needed for work with babies and very young children

---

REFLECTION: FROM PRINCIPLES TO PRACTICE

- What principles do you follow at your setting?

- What principles would you like to add to these, and why?

The sections below expand on each of these principles.

Childhood is a special time to enjoy

The Early Years Foundation Stage (EYFS) in England (DfE, 2017) presents the early years phase of education (from birth to age 5) as a time to get ready for school, equip children with knowledge and skills for life and prepare them for their next steps. The EYFS framework defines its purpose as follows:

> It promotes teaching and learning to ensure children's 'school readiness' and gives children the broad range of knowledge and skills that provide the right foundation for good future progress through school and life.
>
> (DfE, 2017:5)

This emphasis on school readiness has in some way narrowed the focus of early years education and care in England. Providers are encouraged to declare how well children meet pre-set standards in priority subjects such as English and mathematics. Some providers focus their efforts on transmitting knowledge in these areas. Sadly, where providers are led by inexperienced or poorly trained staff, this emphasis can have a detrimental effect on the learning environment and experiences on offer to young children.

REFLECTION: SCHOOL READINESS

■ What do you understand about the term 'school readiness'?

■ How does the emphasis on 'school readiness' affect practice at your setting?

■ Think about a particular child you know well. What sort of environment would support the healthy social and emotional development of this child?

Children learn through play. Play is what children do. It is vital for their healthy emotional, physical, psychosocial and cognitive development (Roberts, 2015). However, as Roberts suggested, some benefits of play, particularly in relation to education, often seem to be valued more in terms of children's *becoming* rather than *being* in the here and now, what it will lead to rather than what can be gained from it in the present.

We, too, hold that play is not only a means to an end, but an end in itself. Play is a source of great enjoyment, an opportunity for children to be expressive, try things out, enact different roles, be themselves, become absorbed, follow their interests and create their own worlds. Childhood, we believe, is a special time in life when children have the right to enjoy the present, be well cared for and nourished in a holistic sense. In other words, it is a time in life to experience the world through all of the senses, a time to grow physically and emotionally, a time to learn to communicate with people, a time to be expressive and creative, and a time to be loved in a very special way.

Children learn about the world through their emotions, their senses and the people around them

There is an increased understanding of how brains are built from pre-birth to around age 8 (Lebedeva, 2015). Adults play a crucial role in building children's brain architecture. This is a momentous responsibility for practitioners in the field. The brain is an organ that is modified through interactions with others. It is crucially important, therefore, that the adults who work with young children understand this.

The brain is made up of four systems:

1 Regulation system
   ■ The brain's chemical messenger system that regulates the body
   ■ Regulation is learned in early childhood, through responsive, consistent and sensitive interactions with others

2 Sensory system
   ■ This system takes sensory information from the environment (e.g. sights, smells) and processes it

3 Relevance system
  ▣ The brain is built up of neural connections
  ▣ Lack of stimulation in early childhood will cut off connections

4 Executive system
  ▣ This system resides in the brain's cortex, or outer layers
  ▣ It is responsible for outward behaviours and dependent on the healthy functioning of the other three systems

(Lebedeva, 2015)

Each of these systems is interconnected and good development in each area is dependent on healthy development in the other areas. Knowledge and understanding of how these systems work may support adults to strengthen their work with individual children. This is not to suggest that adults should adopt a highly scientific approach with children whereby their interventions target particular systems of the brain, but to highlight the importance of knowledge and understanding about brain development in early childhood. This relatively new emphasis on brain development and brain architecture points to the primacy of adult/child relationships in the early years. As Lebedeva underlines, 'relationships are at the core of learning' (2015:22). This is further expanded in Chapter 5 on social learning.

It is important for adults to recognise and encourage children's creative expressions

Children need access to the arts, and adults who have the skills and dispositions to support them in this area. Nutbrown (2013) argued that the arts are central to human development, cognition and well-being, and that a place must be made for the arts in early years curricula. She emphasised the sensory nature of babies, and recommended that, 'from birth, we must seek experiences which smell, or taste, or feel or sound or look pleasing to us, because each of our senses craves satisfaction' (Nutbrown, 2013:241).

This topic is further discussed in Chapter 4 on sensory learning.

REFLECTION: LEARNING THROUGH THE SENSES

▣ What is available in your nursery environment for children to enjoy smelling, tasting, feeling, sounding, listening to or looking at?

▣ Carry out a simple audit to identify any senses that may be underrepresented

▣ What could you offer to develop children's pleasure from these senses?

Creativity may flourish in many forms and all of the art forms can support children's social, emotional and physical development. For example, it is important to tell stories to children and encourage them to participate in them and create their own. There should also be plentiful opportunities for children to listen to and make music. Nutbrown reiterated the message that practitioners should help children engage in the arts. Children should listen to songs, sing songs, compose music. Children should be encouraged to dance. They should be given opportunities to act out familiar stories, stories of their own making and real-life scenarios. Children should have frequent and unhurried opportunities to explore paints and malleable materials, and create sculptures. They should be encouraged to be inventive, make up games, express their ideas.

In our experience, teachers in England frequently lack confidence to teach the arts. They rely on sessional music or dance teachers, for example, and use this time to catch up with planning and paperwork. They often say that the arts are not their speciality.

VIGNETTE: A MUSICAL APPROACH

Sandra, a nursery teacher at a primary school, grew up in a musical family. She has enjoyed making music all her life. She often sings with the children, making up simple songs and rhymes to match children's interests. As a result, children often choose to sing as they play. They make up songs with similar patterns or rhythms to the ones she sings, but which match their current interests. Children in her care have confidence to express themselves and communicate their ideas through music.

■ How do you encourage children to engage in the arts at your setting?

Babies and very young children thrive when they have access to the best integrated care and education

Professor Cathy Nutbrown was commissioned by the government to look into the quality of early years provision in England and her findings were published in 2012 (Nutbrown, 2012). She found that *people* are the most important ingredient in early years education and care. Children's social and emotional well-being and cognitive development, then, are directly related to how well equipped their carers and educators are to support them. The review considered how the training and qualifications system could be developed so that practitioners possessed the necessary skills, knowledge and understanding to provide the best education and care in the early years.

The review confirmed that the best early years practitioners understood, valued and supported young children's play. Importantly, the report suggested that practitioners with higher levels of qualification, and especially those with degree level specialism in early childhood, had the greatest impact on children's learning and development. Graduate professionals, Nutbrown found, made the most difference to the curriculum and to children's outcomes (Cousins, 2016).

Nutbrown pointed to a lack of understanding about the complex and important role early years practitioners undertake. The complexity of work in early years is further explored in Chapter 6 on leadership. Nutbrown emphasised that working with young children involves much more than keeping them clean and well fed, for example. Such misconceptions, Nutbrown suggested, were unhelpful for young children whose needs were often more complex than those of older children.

Not all of the recommendations from the Nutbrown Review were welcomed, and not all found their way into government policy. However, the report made a strong impression on the community of educators, carers, trainers and scholars in England.

Following the Nutbrown Review, the Sutton Trust commissioned a team led by Mathers et al. (2014) at the University of Oxford to carry out a review of research evidence about quality provision for under-three-year-olds in England, and to report on implications on policy and practice. Building on the findings of the Nutbrown Review, this report noted that, in order to deliver this high quality pedagogy, practitioners should be skilled and knowledgeable and able to work within environments which support them in their practice. Staff working with funded two-year-olds, the report recommended, should be qualified to at least Level 3 (or pre-university level) and have support from a graduate practitioner. Furthermore, all practitioners, including childminders, should be able to access qualifications and ongoing professional development, particularly in helping them to meet the needs of disadvantaged children and their families. The report also re-emphasised the point that salaries in the sector should be raised to reflect the requirement for higher qualifications (Mathers et al., 2014: 44).

REFLECTION: TRAINING

- How did your training support you to do your job well?

- What was missing in your training?

- How could training have been improved?

Despite this emphasis on graduate leadership in the early years, another policy briefing about workforce requirements published in 2016 by the Professional

Association for Childcare and Early Years (PACEY) suggested that there was no simple correlation between staff level of education and how well children learn (PACEY, 2016).

The PACEY report acknowledged that the first years of a child's life have a long-term impact on their future health, well-being, and educational attainment. It also emphasised that quality childcare was necessary to support a child's full development, including creativity, curiosity and self-confidence. These were essential conditions for childhood. High quality childcare, it stated, was needed in order to improve children's outcomes, particularly in the areas of cognitive and social development, and to narrow the gap between the most and least disadvantaged children. Unfortunately, the report highlighted that in England, too many children, particularly those living in areas of deprivation, still attended early years settings that lacked sufficiently well-trained and qualified professionals.

In line with the Nutbrown Review (2012) and research by Mathers et al. (2014), the report drew on a number of studies that found quality to be closely associated with qualifications. In England, for example the Effective Pre-School, Primary and Secondary Education Project (Taggart et al., 2015) found a close relationship between higher staff qualifications and higher quality provision. Additionally, according to the regulating body, Ofsted (2015), settings with three-quarters or more of staff qualified to Level 3 or above were found to be significantly more likely to achieve better inspection results than those with less qualified staff.

The PACEY report offered the proviso that qualifications alone were not enough. Rather it was the ability of better qualified practitioners to create a high-quality pedagogic environment in which adults involve children, stimulate interactions with and between children and use diverse scaffolding strategies such as guiding, modelling and questioning (PACEY, 2016). Children need to be engaged in meaningful activities that promote their conceptual understanding of the world. They also need opportunities to develop positive relationships. The PACEY report stated that it was vital to support and improve practitioners' competence to communicate and interact with children.

It was a lack of time and funding, the report concluded, rather than levels of staff motivation, that were the key barriers to developing these effective pedagogic environments. It found that higher qualifications did not necessarily lead to better pay or opportunities. PACEY therefore identified three components as necessary to achieve the best care and education possible for children and their families:

- Professionals committed to continuous improvement

- Access to high quality professional development

- Better recognition in terms of pay and opportunities for the highly skilled work carried out by early years practitioners

The policy briefing recommended that further investment be made in the workforce so that working in the early years was not a less well paid, lower status and less skilled job than working with older children.

Highly skilled and emotionally self-aware people are needed for work with babies and very young children

According to Andrew (2015:360), 'the conditions of work within early childhood are difficult'. Adults in settings play a very important role in supporting children's healthy social and emotional development and preparing them for life. Kultti and Pramling (2015) wrote about the important role early years practitioners have in supporting children's communication and thinking in social contexts. The practitioner's role, they suggested, was to support children to communicate not just about what they saw in the immediate present, but how this related to their past experiences or to contrasting sensual experiences. Kultti and Pramling (2015:107) emphasised the special social learning opportunities available in a nursery or daycare context, which they described as 'a collective arena where children learn in group activities'. In such contexts, the practitioners act as the facilitators.

Other authors have foregrounded the unique opportunities for social learning in nurseries (Dencik, 1989; Dahlberg, Moss and Pence, 2007; Degotardi and Pearson, 2009), arguing that institutional settings offer a qualitatively different, but equally important experience to that offered in familial contexts. Dencik (1989), for example, explained that children in modern Denmark inhabit the *public* world of the nursery, with professional pedagogues who care for them, and the *private* world of the home. Dahlberg et al. (2007:67) challenged the trend in England and the United States for institutions to attempt to replicate the home in some way, with practitioners taking on the role of substitute parents, providing 'close, intimate relationship[s] with the children'. They argued, instead, that out-of-home education and care contexts should not be the same as private, familial contexts. They offer something different, particularly in relation to social learning. Degotardi and Pearson (2009) argued that in out-of-home contexts, such as preschools, children build different sorts of relationships with the different adults and peers they interact with, and experience many different sorts of relationships. These authors wrote about the different experiences and quality of relationships that are afforded in non-familial contexts.

Nurseries and other settings, then, are viewed by some authors as collective arenas where children learn in groups and develop communication skills. Kultti and Pramling (2015:108) defined communication as common, or 'joint sense-making'. This inevitably involves negotiation of understandings to establish intersubjectivity to arrive at shared meanings. They suggested that adults play a crucial role in supporting children to negotiate meanings. Practitioners modelled ways of communicating in less local terms, for example, helping children to draw on and recall different reference points and sensual experiences, thus using words for absent objects or events. Skilled practitioners, they found, allowed children to contribute to evolving understandings about different subject matters in order to communicate effectively with others, drawing on their own social and cultural experiences and perspectives. Skilled practitioners encouraged this collaborative sense-making as part of everyday events such as mealtimes, whereby a simple daily routine might be transformed into 'a pedagogic event' (Kultti and Pramling, 2015:115), so that 'the teacher becomes a participant in activities with children, entering into their sense-making, monitoring and coordinating these into a joint activity where participants learn from and with each other'.

We have established, then, that highly skilled people are needed for this work with babies and very young children. It is also crucially important that adults be emotionally self-aware and well for this work. Page and Elfer (2013:557) argued that early years practitioners need to have been well cared for themselves in order to be able to care for children as they need to be cared for. Practitioners were needed who are not only 'highly qualified', but also 'emotionally resilient'.

Andrew (2015:353) argued that it was important to attend to the 'mental well-being' of early years teachers, and conceived of a framework for this specialist work. Within this, Andrew proposed that work with young children involved more than *episteme*, or knowledge, for example about such areas as child development. It also involved more than *techne*, or technical skills, such as skills to carry out health and safety procedures, manage children's sleep and provide a healthy diet. Andrew (2015:352) suggested that work with young children also drew on *phronesis*, or 'practical wisdom': 'This is everyday knowledge, the logic of practice, which comes from daily engagement with the particular tasks of working with children, and the embodied knowledge that develops as a result.'

Andrew made a strong plea that emotions should not be disregarded as unreliable or inappropriate in this professional work. On the contrary, practitioners should pay close attention to their emotions. They should be encouraged to analyse the resources they draw on to deal with the complexities of their work. They may draw on pre-existing skills, for example, gained from their own experiences of being cared for or caring for others. This informal learning, Andrew argued, should be acknowledged as a valuable resource. Andrew proposed that educators be supported to become conscious of their own emotions and how they manage them and make use of them in their everyday practice.

Andrew recommended that early years practitioners should draw on this practical wisdom as they evaluate what individual children need in different situations. This cannot be prescribed in advance. What works best in particular situations cannot be taken from a field of knowledge or skills base. In other words, 'the book' or 'the manual' cannot contain all the answers. Practitioners need to make judgements based on their life learning, experience in the field, and knowledge of particular children. Importantly, judgements and decisions are made in relationships and within ethical encounters with others. For these reasons, Andrew argues that practical wisdom and moral awareness are needed for this.

REFLECTION: KNOWLEDGE, SKILLS AND WISDOM FOR TEACHING

Identify some examples of how you draw on the following areas of knowledge in your work:

■ Subject knowledge gained from your study

■ Technical skills learned through professional development or as part of your training

■ Practical wisdom learned through life and work experiences

Conclusion

In this chapter we put forward some principles from international, research-based organisations. We introduced our own perspectives on the subject of emotional, sensory and social learning, and presented our set of principles for the book. Each of these principles was elaborated on in turn with reference to research.

The next chapter is about theory. This topic is covered early in the book since it serves as a foundation or underpinning for the ensuing discussions. The practices, policies and perspectives put forward in the book rest on our theoretical positioning. Our thinking is behind everything we write. Additionally, the theories put forward so early in the book may serve to frame some of the discussions and help readers develop their own thinking about the different topics and how they relate to their practice.

After the chapter on theory, each topic in the title of the book is addressed in turn. Chapter 3 is about emotions and love, Chapter 4 about learning through the senses and Chapter 5 about learning in social contexts. Chapter 6 is about leadership, since this is of central importance in making things happen and effecting change as needed. In each chapter we draw on theory and literature to develop discussions. The discussions are interspersed with vignettes from practice to exemplify particular points and show how different practitioners interpret particular theories and policies. Questions are posed after each vignette to encourage readers to develop their own thinking on the topic. Reflection boxes are embedded in each chapter to encourage readers to think about their own practice and how this might be developed.

References

Andrew, Y. (2015) What we feel and what we do: Emotional capital in early childhood work. *Early Years: Journal of International Research & Development*, 35 (4), 351–365. Available from: Education Research Complete, Ipswich, MA.

Center on the Developing Child, Harvard University (2016) *Eight Things to Remember About Child Development*. Online at: developingchild.harvard.edu/resources/8-things-remember-child-development/

Cousins, S. (2016) Policies for quality early years provision. In S. Slaughter (ed.), *Quality in the Early Years*. London: Open University Press.

Dahlberg, G., Moss, P. & Pence, A. (2007) *Beyond Quality in Early Childhood Education and Care: Languages of Evaluation*, 2nd edition. London: Routledge.

Degotardi, S. & Pearson, E. (2009) Relationship theory in the nursery: Attachment and beyond. *Contemporary Issues in Early Childhood*, 10 (2), 144–155.

Dencik, L. (1989) Growing up in a post-modern age: On the child's situation in the modern family, and on the position of the family in the modern welfare state. *Acta Sociologica*, 32 (2), 155–180.

Department for Education (DfE) (2017) *Statutory Framework for the Early Years Foundation Stage*. Online at: www.gov.uk/government/publications

Dowling, M. (2010) Strength of Feeling. *Nursery World* (Haymarket Business Publications Ltd), 3/11/2010, 110 (4210), p. 14–16. Online at: http://www.magonlinelibrary.com/toc/nuwa/2010/3

International Step by Step Association (ISSA) (2016) *Early Years Regional Alliance Manifesto*. Online at: www.earlyyearsregionalalliance.nl

Kultti, A. & Pramling, N. (2015) Limes and lemons: Teaching and learning in preschool as the coordination of perspectives and sensory modalities. *International Journal of Early Childhood*, 47 (1), 105–117.

Lebedeva, G. (2015) Building brains one relationship at a time. *Exchange*, 11, Nov/Dec 2015, 21–25.

Martin, A.D. & Kamberelis, G. (2013) Mapping not tracing: Qualitative educational research with political teeth. *International Journal of Qualitative Studies in Education*, 26 (6), 668–679.

Mathers, S., Eisenstadt, N., Sylva, K., Soukakou, E. & Ereky-Stevens, K. (2014) *Sound Foundations: A Review of the Research Evidence on Quality of Early Childhood Education and Care for Children Under Three*. Oxford: Oxford University and The Sutton Trust.

Murray, L. (2014) *The Psychology of Babies: How Relationships Support Development from Birth to Two*. London: Constable Robinson.

Nutbrown, C. (2012) *Foundations for Quality: The Independent Review of Early Education and Childcare Qualifications*. Online at: www.education.gov.uk

Nutbrown, C. (2013) Conceptualising arts-based learning in the early years. *Research Papers in Education*, 28 (2), 239–263.

Ofsted (2015) *Early Years: The Report of Her Majesty's Chief Inspector of Education, Children's Services and Skills 2015*. Manchester: Ofsted, Online at: www.gov.uk/government/publications/ofsted-early-years-report-2015

Professional Association for Childcare and Early Years (PACEY) (2016) *Towards an Early Years Workforce Development Strategy for England: Policy Briefing*. Online at: https://www.pacey.org.uk/

Page, J. & Elfer, P (2013) The emotional complexity of attachment interactions in nursery. *European Early Childhood Education Research Journal*, 21 (4), 553–567.

Roberts, H. (2015) *Playtime: An Evidence-informed Scoping Review of Children's Play with a Focus on Older Children and Middle Childhood*. Cambridge: Centre for Science and Policy, University of Cambridge.

Rousseau, J. (2000) *Confessions* (A. Scholar Trans.) Oxford: Oxford University Press. (Original work published 1771).

Taggart, B., Sylva, K., Melhuish, E., Sammons, P. & Siraj, I. (2015) *Effective Pre-school, Primary and Secondary Education Project (EPPSE 3–16+)*. UCL Institute of Education, University College London, Birkbeck, University of London, University of Oxford. Online at: http://www.gov.uk/government/publications

Taggart, G. (2011) Don't we care?: The ethics and emotional labour of early years professionalism. *Early Years*, 31 (1), 85–95.

2 Philosophies, frameworks and contemporary perspectives

OVERVIEW OF THE CHAPTER

Some philosophies and theoretical frameworks for investigating emotional, sensory and social learning in early years practice are considered in the first part of this chapter:

■ Philosophical positions of

- Positivism

- Pragmatism

■ Theoretical frameworks

- Postmodernism

- Social constructionism

Some national frameworks to support children's emotional, sensory and social learning are then explored:

■ Early Years Foundation Stage in England

■ *Te Whariki* in New Zealand

■ Early Years Learning Framework in Australia

The final section is about theories and frameworks for research in early childhood:

■ How children develop their own theories about the world

■ Frameworks for early years researchers as put forward by

- Helen Hedges, University of Auckland, New Zealand

- Jane Payler, The Open University, UK; Jan Georgeson, Plymouth University, UK; and Sandie Wong, Charles Sturt University, Australia

Introduction

This chapter is about philosophy, theoretical frameworks and research. It explores what some philosophers say and considers theories that can be used to frame discussions about children's emotional, sensory and social learning. Why is it important to discuss these topics in a book about emotional, sensory and social learning? How do these more esoteric, less accessible topics apply to practice? How can they help us with our work with young children and families?

Thinking about any aspect of education involves philosophical thinking. Educational approaches, such as Steiner, Montessori or Froebel, for example, are built around particular beliefs. Rudolf Steiner (1861–1925) believed in the role of imagination in learning. He established the Waldorf schools to offer a holistic education that focused on the intellectual, practical and artistic development of children. Steiner believed it was important to attend to children's emotional and spiritual development as much as to their cognitive development. These beliefs are still lived out today in numerous Steiner settings throughout the world. This example shows how people feel strongly about their beliefs and want to make them real for others to experience.

As authors of this book, we inevitably write from our own perspectives. Our beliefs, in other words, play an important part in shaping the contents of this book. Burr (2003:152) argued that 'each of us, of necessity, must encounter the world from some perspective or other'. Accordingly, we acknowledge that our own philosophical stances are contained *in* this book, and that, by engaging in a process of defining our own personal beliefs, we are also engaging in philosophical pursuits. Philosophy, we argue, feeds into educational thinking.

In general, we are more comfortable with doubt than certainty, questions than answers, heterogeneity than homogeneity, diverse perspectives than single claims to truth (Cousins, 2015). We resist positivism and draw on pragmatism as a philosophical stance.

On positivism

Emmanuel Kant (1724–1804) emphasised that knowledge is acquired through experience. He argued that there was an enduring substance to be found in things, and that objects had their own unity and identity. This knowledge, Kant argued, could not be gained through reason, but rather through people's experiences of living in the world. Kant argued that grounded knowledge and people's understanding of events and things were more significant than reason, and downplayed the primacy of reason and metaphysical ideas.

Kant developed the principle of universal causality, whereby every thing or happening has a cause. This principle could not be applied as a result of any belief, but only *acquired* as a result of people's experiences in the world. Kant's ideas about cause and effect, the primacy of epistemological knowledge over metaphysical beliefs, and objects as having a permanent substance, may be understood as a precursor to positivism.

The notion of 'positivism' was first conceived of by August Comte (1798–1857). From a positivist perspective, Comte argued, human reason was able to understand how the world worked, or make sense of it. Positivism went through a series of iterations as it developed through history; logical positivism was one such iteration in the 1920s and 1930s whereby empirical materials were converted into knowledge through a process of logical analysis. A century later, positivist perspectives continue to emphasise the importance of investigating observable phenomena to arrive at true knowledge.

The important point to note is that positivism, as a philosophical stance, is associated with a preference for naming and grouping things, ordering events, acknowledging that there is certainty in things and establishing firm structures.

Positivism and emotional, sensory and social learning in the early years

Work in the field of early years calls for an open stance in relation to learning. Practitioners may draw on a range of theories, as promoted in their particular cultures. They may develop stories to make sense of particular children's emotional, sensory and social learning or write highly informative reports about children's development in these areas at particular points in time. Early years practitioners in England are often required to name and define things. They may say that this child is at this stage of development, or displays symptoms of that impairment, for example. Such practices might be associated with positivism.

In this book, by contrast, we advocate an approach whereby practitioners remain open to multiple possibilities, acknowledge that they do not necessarily have the answers, and are ready to be surprised by the unexpected. For example, there are a range of different explanations and theories about how children learn, and different reasons why particular children may behave in particular ways in different contexts. Additionally, there are unknown factors that may affect children's development at different times. In such unchartered landscapes, we suggest, it is advisable for early years practitioners to adopt a non-positivist stance in their work and remain open to multiple possibilities and as yet un-thought-of scenarios. The non-positivist practitioner, for example, may not be able to point to a specific reason why a particular child may be making unexpectedly good progress in the area of social development. Nevertheless, the practitioner may be able to say that they have got to know the child, developed a relationship of mutual trust and appreciation, and that this in turn has led the child to make progress. The practitioner may have entered into a sort of dance with the child (Elfer, Goldschmied and Selleck, 2012). Perhaps they have established a loving relationship with the child, and this in turn has allowed the child to explore further, and venture forth in their learning. From these perspectives, we argue, we cannot draw on positivism to support our thinking about practice.

On pragmatism

We have put forward our position whereby nothing is certain in this world, things change, the unexpected occurs, life happens in unplanned ways, definitions do not hold for all time. We now turn to some formal critiques of positivism and put forward the notion of pragmatism.

The philosopher Bertrand Russell (1912) argued against the positivist yearning for knowledge. Richard Rorty (1931–2007), too, battled against any position that neglected 'the fragile and transitory' (Rorty, 1991:34). Richardson and St Pierre (2005:476), in their writings about research, stated their belief that 'having a partial, local and historical knowledge is still knowing', and that 'there is always more to know' (Ibid.:479).

Russell (1912:242) declared that his aim as a philosopher was 'to keep alive that speculative interest in the universe which is apt to be killed by confining ourselves to definitely ascertainable knowledge'. He emphasised the importance of remaining open to many possibilities and accepting doubt. Such dispositions, he said, free people from 'the tyranny of custom' (Russell, 1912:243). Rorty (1991:33) described positivistic arguments as 'just so many power plays'. He drew on the philosophical works of Heidegger (1889–1976) to emphasise 'the fragility and riskiness of any human project' (Rorty, 1991:34), and wrote that 'Only when we escape from the verificationist impulse to ask "How can we tell a right answer when we hear one?" are we asking questions which Heidegger thinks worth asking' (Ibid.:44).

Pragmatism, then, does not seek to verify things but only to acknowledge the human, transitory nature of all that is and occurs. We find this a particularly useful stance when considering the diverse needs of individual children. Pragmatism as a philosophical framework rests comfortably with the view that children's lives are complex. Similarly, what practitioners may think is best for children is limited by what they know about child development, their observations of children, what families have said about their children, and their own personal and professional experiences with children. Pragmatic practitioners therefore adopt a learning stance, and acknowledge that there is more to know, and children may surprise them.

For the pragmatist, the world out there is not a once-and-for-all given, but is, rather, shaped by the people who perceive it and act in it, in specific contexts and circumstances (Cousins, 2015). The pragmatist has given up 'the neurotic Cartesian quest for certainty' (Rorty, 1982:161), lost hope in the idea of 'permanence' (Ibid.:166), ceased attempts to '[get] things right' or to arrive at a general rule for what makes something good. The pragmatist acknowledges that 'there are no methods for knowing *when* one has reached the truth' (Ibid.:166) (Rorty's emphasis), and that there are only 'transitory human projects' in a complex world.

For the pragmatist, people live in a world built up over time by the communities to which they belong. As Rorty wrote:

> Our identification with our community – our society, our political tradition, our intellectual heritage – is heightened when we see this community as ours rather than nature's, shaped rather than found, one among many which men have made.

(Rorty, 1982:166)

This is a pivotal statement in the context of this book since it emphasises the contextual nature of everything. Children's emotional, sensory and social learning is shaped by the emotional, sensory and social contexts in which they have grown up. People construct their knowledge and ideas with reference to the cultural and social resources at their disposal.

Rorty points to some of the criticisms of pragmatism, including that it is 'frivolous' (1982:172), and has too many 'contingent starting points' (Ibid.:173). In defence of pragmatism, however, we celebrate its practical, worldly stance. Unlike Platonic thinkers who strive to 'escape from conversation to something atemporal which lies in the background' (Ibid.:174), or who prefer to engage in theoretical conversations, pragmatists acknowledge their situated-ness in the world. From their worldly, entangled stance, they see the complexity, contingency and impermanence of all worldly matters. In other words, pragmatists accept that there is no blueprint for how children learn emotionally, through their senses or socially. How children learn is based on a myriad of different historical, physical and cultural contexts. Learning is contextual, mysterious, different for every child.

Pragmatism and emotional, sensory and social learning in the early years

Skilled and intuitive early years practitioners, whether knowingly or not, adhere to such a pragmatic stance. Pragmatic practitioners are ongoing learners, aware that what they learned as part of their training or professional development may no longer hold. The beliefs they once held may have been superseded by new beliefs arising from new research, or improved practices drawing on refreshed or widened perspectives. The world keeps moving and these pragmatic practitioners are aware of the need to keep contributing to this movement, as well as moving with it.

Pragmatic practitioners embrace rather than resist change. They welcome new perspectives, and remain open to their own learning. Pragmatic practitioners perceive themselves as ongoing learners. They learn from scholarship, personal reflections, experience and observations of individual children. Pragmatic practitioners are lifelong learners.

On postmodernism

In this section we consider the notion of postmodernism, and how it connects to pragmatism. In postmodernism, as Gergen (1991:7) defined the notion, there is no certainty or predictability about things, and, instead 'the centre fails to hold'. Gergen (1999:7) suggested that, in postmodernism, everything people talk about points more to their perspectives than to anything substantial: 'In the postmodern world we become increasingly aware that the objects about which we speak are not so much "in the world" as they are products of perspective'.

The world is unstable and open to reconstruction. This serves to remind us that what we write about how children learn emotionally, through their senses and socially, will represent our particular perspectives, and that these perspectives may change or be given different emphases in the future or in different political or cultural contexts. In a postmodern world, beliefs do not necessarily hold and ideas do not correspond to things. As Gergen (1991:7) wrote, 'under postmodern conditions, persons exist in a continuous construction and reconstruction; it is a world where anything goes that can be negotiated'. Postmodernists do not apply criteria such as reason or truth, but look for such things as 'emotionality, personal responsibility, an ethic of caring ... and dialogues with subjects' (Denzin and Lincoln, 2003:15). Truths, from this perspective, are temporary constructions, constructed within relationships, in dialogue with others, and applicable within the specific contexts in which they arise.

Deleuze and Guattari (1994:144) complemented this postmodern stance. For these authors, 'concepts have no reference to the lived or states of affairs'. Foucault (1972), too, challenged the notion that there was anything beyond language, and as Rorty (1986:48) wrote in his critique of Foucault's theories, he believed that 'we only know the world and ourselves under a description'. From a postmodern perspective, talk does not refer to real things, but is how people communicate with others in their communities, construct stories and make meaning. Language grounds or locates people within particular socio-cultural environments, and constructs new and impermanent realities. Rorty (1982, 1986) argued that language evolves with reference to people's needs and desire to express themselves, and is developed out of people's cultural and social circumstances. Language, then, like culture, which, according to Williams (1976), comes from the Latin word *cultura*, associated with tending crops or animals, grows slowly.

Deleuze and Guattari (1994:97) proposed that thinking is a form of experimentation, allowing new things to take shape. They wrote that things happen 'as a result of contingency rather than necessity ... of becoming rather than history ... of a grace rather than a nature'. In other words, these authors acknowledged that there are no simple answers and explanations for things. In pragmatism, too, there is no certainty in the world, or any script for people to follow; instead there is scope to be creative, and for 'acts which let new sorts of being be' (Rorty, 1991:46). For the pragmatist, the world is not only fragile, risky and unpredictable, but also full of possibilities. Similarly, from a postmodern perspective, things come into being and cannot always be predicted; they are born, mysteriously, and may not have been written in any script (Cousins, 2015).

Postmodernism and emotional, sensory and social learning in the early years

In the context of this book, this is an invitation to the reader to remain open to possibilities about how children learn. There may be positivist pressures for practitioners to measure children's progress against pre-defined curricular frameworks or assessment scales. However, we propose that practitioners be encouraged to consider how children learn in ways that are unexpected and surprising, and in ways that do not necessarily fit into pre-defined models of learning. Every child learns in their own unique way and along previously untrodden pathways. Educators and carers of very young children, from our perspectives, are privileged to witness daily marvels and surprises.

REFLECTION: UNEXPECTED LEARNING

▪ Think about a child's learning that was unexpected or surprising

▪ Based on your knowledge of the child and their family, what might have contributed to this?

▪ How does this unexpected learning inform your practice?

Social constructionism

In this section we discuss the theoretical framework of social constructionism. According to Burr (2003), social constructionism is built on the belief that meaning is constructed, not something that is fixed. Meaning is open to diverse interpretations depending on how messages are communicated and by whom, and also on who receives them. Meaning 'is fluid, volatile and always open to change through the medium of social interaction' (Burr, 2003:44). It is not definitive for all time or conclusive.

Many different meanings are constructed by different people. Gergen (1999:17) suggested that by accepting one meaning as definitive, or by holding firm to a particular interpretation, other possibilities are inevitably discarded. He wrote that 'as we presume the reality and truth of our beliefs, so do we trample on the beliefs of others'.

From a social constructionist perspective, then, we acknowledge that there are multiple possibilities to be considered, where people draw on their experiences of being in the world to construct meaning. This is not to say that a social constructionist framework adopts a deterministic stance, such that people are indelibly influenced or shaped by their past experiences. There is no *inevitability* within a social constructionist framework. So, although people *draw* on their social and cultural resources, they are not *determined* by them (Cousins, 2015).

A social constructionist framework is suitable for areas involving people. Accordingly, we do not write this book as avatars (Cousins, 2015), with no feelings, but as living persons in the world. Unlike a scientific book in which topics may be reported in a more objective, detached way, we acknowledge that we are unable to 'stand back from [our] own humanity' (Burr, 2003:151), and that what we write is constructed with reference to our own experiences in different social, emotional and cultural resources.

There are some problems associated with social constructionism. Firstly, there is the problem of language. Some authors (Richardson, 1990; Denzin, 2010; Bochner, 2014) have argued that words do not correspond to actual events or things in the material world. Barad (2003:881) argued that words cannot be 'tethered' to anything real, and St Pierre (2013:649) proposed that, since there is no 'reality out there to be found out', language could never represent anything accurately. If these ideas are accepted, then it should also be acknowledged that there is uncertainty and transience to any verbal or written account, and all that exists are other people's accounts, drawing on their social and cultural resources. There is a problem with this position. If nothing can be agreed on in relation to things, how can strategies be developed to support children to learn better?

In some ways, this may be a problem. How can situations such as poverty, injustice or abuse ever be addressed? People talk about poverty, for example, from their diverse perspectives. When some people say they are too poor to afford certain things, therefore, they may not mean 'poor' in the same way as others understand the term. They may, in fact, be materially quite well off. Accordingly, a social constructionist framework may lead us to wonder what may be done about anything at all, if all there is are the things people say and the meanings they exchange. We are also forced to consider where and precisely what the object of study is so that solutions can be identified and closely targeted. This is a problem for anyone who strives to get to the bottom of things in order to understand them and propose solutions that are well matched to the issues at hand (Cousins, 2015).

Another issue to be aware of with social constructionism, particularly in relation to the topic of emotional, sensory and social learning, is the use of these concepts in themselves. Words have many meanings. The question of whether words can ever adequately convey the complexity of concepts such as emotional learning needs to be considered. However, even though the concepts of emotional, sensory and social learning are complex and contain disparate meanings, we have chosen to focus on these topics since we believe they are important.

Social constructionism and emotional, sensory and social learning

It is helpful for practitioners to be aware of the problems with language. What an early years framework or policy prescribes, or what a piece of early years research finds, for example, cannot be viewed as applicable in all contexts or helpful for all time. All that is said, both in writing and in current discourse, is interpreted variously according to the context in which it takes place. Meaning is constructed from different perspectives, and meaning changes.

For example, although some authors (Elfer et al., 2012; Page, 2011) argue that it is important for children's healthy emotional development to form close attachments with practitioners in non-familial settings, other authors (Dencik, 1989; Dahlberg, Moss and Pence, 2007; Degotardi and Pearson, 2009) argue that it is not (see Chapter 3). Thus perspectives differ, and these differences are reflected in different constructions.

Early years priorities and emphases also change over time. For example, the psychologist Winnicott (1964) wrote that someone in a professional caring role should adopt a very different role to that of a parent: 'She has, in contrast to the mother, technical knowledge derived from her training, and an attitude of objectivity towards the children under her care' (1964:195).

Winnicott emphasised the more technical role and objective approach to be adopted in non-familial, education and care contexts. In more recent work, however, this emphasis has changed. Researchers highlight the importance of forming close relationships with children in out-of-home contexts, especially since many children are in daycare or nurseries while their parents work (Page, 2011; Elfer et al., 2012).

As economic or social contexts change, then, so priorities shift to accommodate new needs. Additionally, new research renders previous constructions less relevant or less reliable. For example, scholars at Harvard University stated as one of their principles that while young children's attachments to their parents are primary, they can also benefit significantly from relationships with other responsive caregivers outside the family (Center on the Developing Child, 2016).

Half a century on, then, Winnicott's perspective from the 1960s no longer holds as much credence. Beliefs change. Positions shift.

Frameworks to support children's emotional, sensory and social learning

In the sections above we considered philosophical perspectives and frameworks to support practitioners' thinking about learning. In the sections below we explore some international frameworks for early years practice and how some contemporary thinkers have developed theoretical frameworks to underpin work in this field.

The Early Years Foundation Stage Framework in England (DfE, 2017) was developed in 2007 to establish a principled approach, so that practical guidance was underpinned by research. According to the framework, the four guiding principles that should shape practice are:

- Every child is a **unique child**, who is constantly learning and who can be resilient, capable, confident and self-assured

- Children learn to be strong and independent through **positive relationships**

- Children learn and develop well in **enabling environments**, in which their experiences respond to their individual needs, and there is a strong partnership between practitioners and parents and/or carers

- **Children develop and learn in different ways and at different rates**. The framework covers the education and care of all children in early years provision, including children with special educational needs and disabilities
(DfE, 2017:6)

Since 2012 the government added a further model of effective learning and teaching to support practitioners in their work with young children. The revised documentation stated that practitioners must reflect on the ways that children learn, and adapt their practice accordingly. The 'characteristics of effective learning' were defined as:

- **Playing and exploring** – children investigate and experience things, and 'have a go'

- **Active learning** – children concentrate and keep on trying if they encounter difficulties, and enjoy achievements

- **Creating and thinking critically** – children have and develop their own ideas, make links between ideas, and develop strategies for doing this
(DfE, 2017:10)

In addition to these principles and characteristics, the government identified seven areas of learning, including 'personal, social and emotional development'. Under this area, for example, practitioners should help children to:

- Develop a positive sense of themselves, and others

- Form positive relationships and develop respect for others

- Develop social skills and learn how to manage their feelings

- Understand appropriate behaviour in groups

- Have confidence in their own abilities

(DfE, 2017:8)

The idea of a framework such as this one is that practitioners should base their work on research-informed principles, meet different curriculum statements, and evaluate their work with reference to agreed characteristics of effective learning and teaching. Thus different strands are woven together to build coherence and strengthen practice.

Of course, there are political drivers at work behind this and all other frameworks. Some might argue, for example, that the idea of 'school readiness' lies behind the curriculum requirement for children to understand appropriate behaviour in groups. Children should learn to cooperate in groups so that the Key Stage 1 curriculum (ages 5 to 7) is effectively transmitted and good outcomes in the core areas of English and mathematics are achieved. Some might argue that this aligns with a broader, neo-liberal perspective whereby education is regarded as necessary for strong economic growth in the future. From this perspective, economics are more important than children's emotional well-being, or social development.

The highly acclaimed *Te Whariki* curriculum from New Zealand adopted a weaving metaphor to convey its four principles:

1 Empowerment

2 Relationships

3 Family and community

4 Holistic development

Five strands were woven through these principles:

1 Well-being

2 Belonging

3 Communication

4 Contribution

5 Exploration

In addition to these strands, a further layer about children's knowledge, skills and attitudes was interwoven to add strength to the framework:

■ Dispositions (approaches to learning)

■ Working theories (thinking skills and capacities)

(Hedges, 2015:84–85)

Hedges (2015:84) described the *Te Whariki* curriculum as: 'a highly participatory series of events, both pre-planned and spontaneous, that arise from interactions, activities and events in which teachers and children engage'.

Thus, the *Te Whariki* framework relies on strong relationships between children and practitioners. It cannot simply be adopted in a performative sense (Osgood, 2006, 2012), unthinkingly, as if by automatons rather than people with agency. On the contrary, it is important that teams interrogate frameworks, consider how they correlate with their own setting or centre principles, and apply them to their own contexts.

Peers and Fleer (2014) emphasised the need for practitioners and researchers to consider the meaning behind the language used in frameworks. For example, with reference to the Australian Early Years Learning Framework (Australian Government Department of Education, Employment and Workplace, 2009), 'belonging' was defined as an experience that was integral to human existence. However, no definition of 'human existence' was provided within the Australian documents. Peers and Fleer argued that this was an important omission, and that terms and phrases adopted in the framework should be explored in depth. Terms like belonging were highly complex and this complexity needed to be explored in full. Peers and Fleer (2014:924) suggested, for example, that the notion of 'belonging' was 'the in-between-ness a child may be experiencing in play as a twofold-ness or interconnecting of different states'. When children played a game about dogs, for example, they might feel happiness and fear at the same time. Peers and Fleer emphasised that play is a highly complex pursuit in which children coexist alongside others and in relation to others, but are also separate from others. The language of frameworks, these researchers recommended, needed to be fully explored in order to support practice effectively.

REFLECTION: FRAMEWORKS FOR PRACTICE

■ How do frameworks support your work with young children and their families?

■ How do you use frameworks to establish a coordinated, whole team approach?

■ What, if anything, is missing from the frameworks you use?

Theoretical frameworks developed by children and early years researchers

Frameworks such as the Early Years Foundation Stage in England, the Early Years Learning Framework in Australia, or the *Te Whariki* approach in New Zealand have been developed to support practice. They have been constructed by 'experts' to provide succinct overviews of what was involved in good practice, with different dimensions, layers and perspectives.

Theoretical frameworks work on a further level. From the *Te Whariki* perspective, for example, children develop their own theories about the world. Indeed, they are encouraged to think creatively about the world, and this in turn boosts their self-esteem and independence (Hedges, 2015). Children can come to perceive themselves as full participants in the world, and creators of new theories, rather than as passive participants, or as children in waiting, who learn only from the theories developed by adults. *Te Whariki* is, in this sense, a thoroughly participatory model.

Frameworks, then, are helpful and can strengthen practice. However, as emphasised in this chapter, frameworks also need to be carefully critiqued by skilled and knowledgeable practitioners. In Chapter 1 we explored the need for practitioners to be well-trained, intuitive and emotionally mature for this complex work in early years. With reference to the concept of 'funds of knowledge' (Moll et al., 1992, cited in Hedges, 2015), for example, a practitioner may dutifully apply a socio-cultural approach to their work, attentive to what children already know and understand from their family and cultural contexts. Early years practitioners may make it their business to get to know families and build on what children already know from their home contexts. But this in itself may not be enough. Hedges (2015) argued the need to critique this 'funds of knowledge' approach. For example:

- Is it appropriate for practitioners to select which funds of knowledge should be celebrated and which should be neglected, such as funds of knowledge related to violence and crime?

- What is the role of practitioners in fostering children's critical thinking about stereotypes, e.g. gender stereotypes?

- Should practitioners help children understand that there are other cultural repertoires adopted in other contexts?

Funds of knowledge, Hedges pointed out, may also be learned in settings, in relationships with practitioners and other children. All of these questions and layers need to be considered by practitioners.

The main point is that theoretical frameworks cannot be applied as if from a 'How to ...' manual, but adopted wholeheartedly, built on and extended by reflective practitioners in relation to their experience and observations of individual children.

HEDGES' RESEARCH ABOUT SOPHIA IN RELATION TO HER BROTHER SAMUEL, AND HER GENDER-RELATED WORKING THEORY

'Sophia … expressed strong ideas about gender roles involved in caring for children. On one occasion, she prevented Samuel from placing a doll into a baby carrier, telling him that:

> Only mummies are allowed to carry the babies. Daddy isn't allowed to carry the babies.

> Daddy's job is to go to work. … Mummy and Nana's job to look after baby.
> (FN/45)

In this way, Sophia's funds of knowledge had led her to form a gender-related working theory about caring for infants that she acted on, thereby likely reinforcing and influencing Samuel's views of accepted roles and practices across contexts too.'

(Hedges, 2015:89)

As a result of this research, Hedges recommended that practitioners be attentive to the complexity of learning in social contexts. Learning in families, communities and settings is complex, and all aspects need to be carefully considered by committed and deeply reflective practitioners. There are no simple explanations about how children learn, theories that can be applied, or frameworks that fit. The world is messy, with multiple challenges and no clear solutions.

This, of course, echoes closely the philosophical position of pragmatism and theoretical framework of postmodernism explored earlier in this chapter. The world is in flux, and there are multiple ways of understanding different components within it, and how they connect to other components. Working with very young children is highly complex.

Theoretical frameworks for inclusive research

This emphasis on the complexity of work in early years was taken up by Payler, Georgeson and Wong (2016) in their research on interprofessional practice. The researchers noted that, given the lower status of early years professionals when compared to professionals in other children's services, it was particularly important to analyse and delineate the work they did. The researchers focused on support for children with special educational needs and disabilities.

They established a framework for research into interprofessional practice, involving early years practitioners, other professionals, children and families. They found that understanding about children was enhanced by adopting a multifaceted approach. Practitioners learned about children over time and in dialogue with parents and other practitioners. It was important for practitioners and researchers alike to be attentive to children's bodily and vocal communication, especially since children express their feelings, interests and wishes in these ways.

EXAMPLE OF A CHILD AND THEIR ATTENTIVE ADULT DEVELOPING A RELATIONALLY RESPONSIVE FORM OF UNDERSTANDING

'His developing relationship with his key person, her mediation and the speech therapy he had (which his key person also attended) were all contributing to enabling him to participate more fully and make greater use of verbal communication. Gradually he had begun to interact more and his key person's sensitive responses helped to ensure that progress was effective and at his pace, helping to build his trust and motivation to communicate. She acted as a broker to his communication with other children.

> I've seen him go up to a child and look at what that child has in his hand and then he'll come up to me and drag me to the child and I'm so excited about this. Daniel is not giving that child any eye contact, but the child gave the toy to Daniel and he had a great big smile on his face. That made Daniel happy, made the child happy and made me ecstatic as that's the first step to communication with that child.
>
> [(key person).]'

(Payler, Georgeson and Wong, 2016:21)

This evidence from Payler, Georgeson and Wong's research points to the rewarding and highly skilled nature of work with very young children. When a practitioner helps a child to take a significant step in their learning they may feel a sense of great satisfaction. This accords with a body of research on the positive aspects of emotional labour in early years (Lynch, Baker and Lyons, 2009; Boyer, Reimer and Irvine, 2012).

Payler et al. (2016) recommended that researchers attend closely to children's communication and support them to participate in different social contexts.

They suggested the following guiding principles for understanding and learning from young children's participation in interprofessional practice:

1 Attend to the situated, responsive actions of *all* participants

2 Attend to *affect* and the fine-grained detail of bodily enactments of affect as part of those actions

3 *Evidence* the vocalised and bodily expressed cognitive, social, physical and emotional responses of dialogic communication between participants

4 *Contextualise* and reflect on the evidence through the attention to trajectories of participation in and between other contexts; and through attention to others' interpretations of the evidence

5 Develop identify shifting, shared *understanding* in situ and over time between participants

(Payler et al., 2016:23)

Research in early years, and from this perspective, then, is highly skilled work. If it is to be of any value, it involves close work and finely tuned skills of observation and attention, and wide knowledge and understanding about how children learn in different contexts.

Conclusion

In this chapter we put forward some philosophical and theoretical frameworks for practice and research, particularly in relation to young children's emotional, sensory and social learning. We argued why we resisted *positivism* and chose to lean, instead, on *pragmatism*. We explored the theoretical frameworks of *postmodernism* and *social constructionism* and made links with practice. National frameworks were considered as well as frameworks developed by scholars for research in this area. Frameworks may work for leaders, practitioners, children and researchers. They exist to support practice. However, frameworks should not be adopted unthinkingly, but critiqued and developed by all stakeholders.

The following chapter considers the emotional aspect of work in early years and argues that love is important for children's healthy social and emotional development.

References

Australian Government Department of Education, Employment and Workplace (2009) *Belonging, Being and Becoming: The Early Years Learning Framework for Australia.*

Barad, K. (2003) Posthumanist performativity towards an understanding of how matter comes to matter. *Signs*, (3), 801.

Bochner, A.P. (2014) *Coming to Narrative: A Personal History of Paradigm Change in the Human Sciences.* Walnut Creek, CA, USA: Left Coast Press.

Boyer, K., Reimer, S. & Irvine, L. (2012) The nursery workspace, emotional labour and contested understandings of commoditized childcare in the contemporary UK. *Social and Cultural Geography*, 14 (5), 517–540.

Burr, V. (2003) *Social Constructionism*, 2nd edition. Hove: Routledge.

Center on the Developing Child, Harvard University (2016) *Eight Things to Remember About Child Development.* Online at: developingchild.harvard.edu/resources/8-things-remember-child-development/

Cousins, S. (2015) *Practitioners' Constructions of Love in the Context of Early Childhood Education and Care: A Narrative Inquiry* (Unpublished EdD research thesis, University of Sheffield, Sheffield). Online at: http://etheses.whiterose.ac.uk/8855/

Dahlberg, G., Moss, P. & Pence, A. (2007) *Beyond Quality in Early Childhood Education and Care: Languages of Evaluation*, 2nd edition. London: Routledge.

Degotardi, S. & Pearson, E. (2009) Relationship theory in the nursery: Attachment and beyond. *Contemporary Issues in Early Childhood*, 10 (2), 144–155.

Deleuze, G. & Guattari, F. (1994) *What is Philosophy?* London: Verso.

Dencik, L. (1989) Growing up in a post-modern age: On the child's situation in the modern family, and on the position of the family in the modern welfare state. *Acta Sociologica*, 32 (2), 155–180.

Denzin, N.K. (2010) Moments, mixed methods and paradigm dialogs. *Qualitative Inquiry*, 16 (6), 419–429.

Denzin, N.K. & Lincoln, Y.S. (eds) (2003) *Strategies of Qualitative Inquiry*, 2nd edition. Thousand Oaks, CA, USA: Sage.

Department for Education (DfE) (2017) *Statutory Framework for the Early Years Foundation Stage.* Online at: www.gov.uk/government/publications

Elfer, P., Goldschmied, E. & Selleck, D.Y. (2012) *Key Persons in the Early Years: Building Relationships for Quality Provision in Early Years Settings and Primary Schools*, 2nd edition. Abingdon: Routledge.

Foucault, M. (1972) *The Archaeology of Knowledge* (A.M. Sheridan Smith Trans.). London: Routledge Classics. (Original work published 1969).

Gergen, K.J. (1991) *The Saturated Self: Dilemmas of Identity in Contemporary Life.* USA: Basic Books.

Gergen, K.J. (1999) *An Invitation to Social Construction.* London: Sage.

Hedges, H. (2015) Sophia's funds of knowledge: Theoretical and pedagogical insights, possibilities and dilemmas. *International Journal of Early Years Education*, 23 (1), 83–96.

Lynch, K., Baker, J. & Lyons, M. (2009) *Affective Equality: Love, Care and Injustice.* Basingstoke: Palgrave Macmillan.

Moll, L.C., Amanti, C., Neff, D. & Gonzalez, N. (1992) Funds of knowledge for teaching: Using a qualitative approach to connect homes and classrooms. *Theory into Practice* 31 (2), 132–141.

Osgood, J. (2006) Deconstructing professionalism in early childhood education: Resisting the regulatory gaze. *Contemporary Issues in Early Childhood*, 7 (1), 5–14.

Osgood, J. (2012) *Narratives from the Nursery: Negotiating Professional Identities in Early Childhood.* Abingdon: Routledge.

Page, J. (2011) Do mothers want professional carers to love their babies? *Journal of Early Childhood Research*, 1 (14), 1–14.

Payler, J., Georgeson, J. & Wong, S. (2016) Young children shaping interprofessional practice in early years settings: Towards a conceptual framework for understanding experiences and participation. *Learning Culture and Social Interactions*, 8, 12–24.

Peers, C. & Fleer, M. (2014) The theory of 'Belonging': Defining concepts used within Belonging, Being and Becoming – The Australian Early Years Learning Framework. *Educational Philosophy and Theory*, 41 (8), 914–928.

Richardson, L. (1990) *Writing Strategies: Reaching Diverse Audiences*. Newbury Park, USA: Sage Publications.

Richardson, L. & St Pierre, E.A. (eds) (2005) Writing: A method of inquiry. In N.K. Denzin & Y. Lincoln (eds), *Handbook of Qualitative Research*, 3rd edition (pp. 959–978). Thousand Oaks, CA, USA: Sage.

Rorty, R. (1982) *Consequences of Pragmatism*. Minneapolis, MN, USA: University of Minnesota Press.

Rorty, R. (1986) Foucault and epistemology. In D.C. Hoy (ed.), *Foucault: A Critical Reader* (pp. 41–50). Oxford: Basil Blackwell.

Rorty, R. (1991) *Essays on Heidegger and Others: Philosophical Papers. Volume 2.* Cambridge: Cambridge University Press.

Russell, B. (1912) *The Problems of Philosophy*. London: Thornton Butterworth.

St Pierre, E.A. (2013) The posts continue: Becoming. *International Journal of Qualitative Studies in Education*, 26 (6), 645–657.

Williams, R. (1976) *Keywords: A Vocabulary of Culture and Society*. London: Fontana Press.

Winnicott, D.W. (1964) *The Child, the Family, and the Outside World*. Harmondsworth: Penguin Books.

3 Emotions and love

OVERVIEW OF THE CHAPTER

This chapter is about the emotional aspect of work in early childhood contexts. The following topics are considered:

- Focus on emotions and emotional well-being in early childhood, and why this is important

- Play and emotional well-being

- Love in early childhood

- Historical constructions of love in early childhood

- Training for emotional aspects of work

- The notion of attachment

- The benefits of practitioners reflecting on their practice

- Connections between the physical environment and children's healthy emotional development

Introduction

This chapter focuses on learning through the emotions. We adopt the view that emotions are a form of knowing the world (Janks, 2010). In other words, children develop an emotional blueprint made up of associations between their physical and sensory experiences and feelings. They build up an emotional map that correlates with how they felt in different contexts and with different people. What does research say about emotional learning? How is emotional well-being, for example, different from being loved, or healthily attached to an adult? How can early years practitioners make provision for children's emotional learning?

Who can support children's emotional learning? How should the environment be organised to support emotional learning? How emotionally well do early years practitioners need to be to do this work?

Why is it important to focus on emotions?

Some children in England have been found to be particularly unhappy. International studies have shown that around 10 per cent of children in England experience low levels of well-being and need support (The Children's Society, 2015). This is something that early years practitioners need to be attentive towards, since the sooner children are supported in this area, the more likely they are to grow up emotionally well.

Studies (Bos et al., 2011) of children in Romanian orphanages from the late twentieth century have identified negative effects on mental health of children who experienced early institutional care. These studies also confirmed the increased advantages of early family placement for children living in institutions. Babies and children in orphanages did not have access to warm, responsive, loving adults. They displayed signs of sadness, resigned to the fact that no one would respond to their calls for help, meet their physical or emotional needs, or share their expressions of joy. Attending to the emotional needs of babies and very young children, then, is vitally important.

Emotional well-being is now widely acknowledged as crucial. The Special Educational Needs and Disability (SEND) Code of Practice (Dfe and DoH, 2015) in England points to the range of special educational needs and/or disabilities associated with children's emotional development. From an early age, children may become withdrawn, for example. They may display challenging, disruptive or disturbing behaviour. These behaviours may reflect underlying mental health difficulties such as early indications of anxiety or depression. The code stipulates that early years teams should have clear processes to support children, and one of the ways in which this can be achieved is through an effective key person approach. The key person, or professional assigned to a particular child, offers emotional and practical support as part of a trusting relationship. (This approach is discussed further in the section on attachment and in Chapter 5).

This section emphasised the importance of attending to children's emotional development. The different meanings of emotion, emotional well-being, love and attachment are considered in the sections below.

What is emotion and emotional well-being?

The experiential aspect of emotion is emphasised by Madrid, Fernie and Kantor (2014). Every emotion felt is correlated with a lived experience. Emotions, these authors suggest, are what children experience on a daily basis. They are negotiated between children and adults throughout the day, every day. And yet, as Wilson and Wilson (2015) argue, 'emotion' is also a difficult concept to define. Notions of emotional learning intersect with notions of cognitive and social learning. According to Wilson and Wilson, there are different theories on emotions, but no unified approach exists as yet. Emotions are subjective feelings and there is a distinction between primary or basic emotions and secondary emotions. According to Wilson and Wilson, primary emotions are universal and innate, whereas secondary emotions are culturally specific, developed in diverse ways and are of different intensities. In other words, things can go wrong when children are faced with adverse circumstances. So, although emotion is widely acknowledged to be important in early years education and care contexts, it is a complex notion with multiple strands and meanings.

The notion of emotional well-being was explored in a comprehensive literature review by Weare (2015). According to Weare, social and emotional well-being refers to

> a state of positive mental health and wellness. It involves a sense of optimism, confidence, happiness, clarity, vitality, self-worth, achievement, having a meaning and purpose, engagement, having supportive and satisfying relationships with others and understanding oneself, and responding effectively to one's own emotions.
>
> (Weare, 2015:3)

The social aspects of learning are explored in Chapter 5. The emotional elements within Weare's definition point to the need for children to feel positive, happy and alive. Children who are emotionally well, from this perspective, have an urge to explore the world. They interact with others confidently, and are aware of their own feelings.

REFLECTION: EMOTIONAL WELL-BEING

Consider the emotional well-being of a child you know with reference to Weare's definition.

- How does the child communicate a sense of optimism?

- How does the child display confidence?

- What evidence do you observe that the child is happy?

- Give examples of how the child shows a sense of self-worth

- What does the child do or say to express a sense of achievement?

- How engaged is the child in their learning?

- Is there anything you could add to Weare's definition to indicate well-being?

Weare's definition is echoed in the national framework (DfE, 2017). As specified in the early learning goals for the prime area of personal, social and emotional development, children should be confident in trying new activities, speaking in familiar groups, making choices about what they want to do and asking for support when they need it. Further, children should be able to talk about feelings, recognise how their behaviour might affect the feelings of others, adjust their behaviour to different situations, and be able to adapt to new situations.

Another use of the word emotion in educational contexts is as part of the phrase 'emotional intelligence'. Emotional intelligence in the context of early childhood refers to children's awareness and ability to control and express their emotions in different contexts. How well are children able to interpret other people's expressions of emotions? Can children distinguish between their own different feelings? How well do children use emotional information to guide their own behaviour? How aware are they that different behaviours and emotional responses are appropriate in different contexts? Emotional intelligence, then, is akin to emotional literacy. It is about how well children interpret emotions and communicate effectively through them. However, the research associated with the notion of emotional intelligence has been highly contested, and the umbrella term was not considered helpful in the context of this book.

Play and emotional well-being

Play is one of the main ways that children learn about themselves and grow emotionally well (Robinson and May, 2014). Early years practitioners need knowledge and understanding about emotional development in order to support children in their play and reflect on their interventions. Skilled practitioners support children to learn through play experiences that are both safe and challenging. They know their children well and understand how they engage in different play experiences. These skilled practitioners also reflect on their own practice, help parents to support their children's learning at home, and provide learning experiences that are appropriate for individual children and allow every child to learn and feel positive about their learning.

According to Roberts (2015), some studies have suggested that children with regular access to natural environments fare particularly well in an emotional sense. According to these studies, traditional locations for adventurous play, including the outdoors and green spaces, support children's mental health and emotional well-being. Studies have emphasised the positive benefits of adventurous play on children's mental health and well-being. Children with Attention Deficit Hyperactivity Disorder (ADHD), for example, experienced reduced symptoms and the emotional development of all children was enhanced. The benefits of outdoor play are explored in more detail in Chapter 5.

REFLECTION: SUPPORTING EMOTIONAL DEVELOPMENT

■ How do you support children's emotional development through play?

■ How do you use the natural environment to support children's emotional development?

What is love in education and care contexts?

The word emotion is closely associated with close relationships. Emotional well-being comes about within positive, warm, loving relationships. These relationships cannot be merely performed by practitioners, but must be experienced by them. The authors of this book adopt the view that close relationships in early years settings and homes involve genuine feelings of love between adults and children.

Over half a century ago Fletcher (1958:118) noted that the word love 'led to a confusion of meanings'. More recently, Page (2011:312) wrote that 'love is not easily defined or discussed'. For Page (2011:316), the concept was 'nebulous'.

This 'confusion of meanings' arises in part since the word love incorporates a range of definitions. Collins Dictionary offers the following definitions:

Verb

1 To have a great attachment to and affection for

2 To have passionate desire, longing, and feelings for

3 To like or desire (to do something) very much

4 To make love

5 To be in love

Noun

6 An intense emotion of affection, warmth, fondness, and regard towards a person or thing

7 A deep feeling of sexual attraction and desire

8 Wholehearted liking for or pleasure in something

9 *(Christianity)*
    a God's benevolent attitude towards man
    b Man's attitude of reverent devotion towards God

(www.collinsdictionary.com/dictionary/English)

The dictionary definition of the verb 'to love' that is most useful in the context of work with babies and very young children is 'to have a great attachment to or affection for' someone. As a noun, the most helpful one is the sixth definition, namely 'an intense emotion of affection, warmth, fondness, and regard towards a person'.

Other definitions are also relevant. Definitions 2, 4, 5 and 7 allude to love in an erotic, sexual sense. Accordingly, they relate to concerns about the potential for child abuse in the context of work in early childhood where adults routinely touch children as part of their 'loving' relationships with them. Love expressed through touch is something that is greatly feared in the context of early childhood education and care in England. There is a 'moral panic' (Piper and Smith, 2003:890) that prevails in relation to the subject of child abuse, reinvigorated with particular force following the Jimmy Savile and Rolf Harris cases of 2012–2014 (Weaver, 2014). The word love, then, encapsulates a range of meanings, and any one of these meanings might be applied in the context of work with babies and very young children.

Dowling (2010) emphasised the importance of love in professional contexts. According to Dowling, although love in settings and homes cannot address all matters, children cannot thrive or learn if they are not loved. Dowling wrote of the importance of professional love. Professional love, for Dowling, meant:

■ Getting to know a child – really getting under her skin

■ Setting boundaries that help a child feel safe rather than restricting her

■ Taking a child seriously and respecting her thoughts and ideas

■ Understanding a child's behaviour while not excusing it

■ Showing the way, through modelling attitudes and actions

■ Sharing something of yourself, your time, patience, ability to listen and your views and experiences

For Dowling, these conditions are possible when practitioners show unconditional regard for children, whereby they love children for who they are, rather than for what they can do and achieve.

History of love in educational contexts

The word love has been used in educational contexts in a variety of senses over the centuries. For example, since 1543, the Jesuit religious order conveyed a belief whereby, when children love their teachers, they are more likely to develop a love for learning (in Lawrence, 1970:63); Roger Ascham (1515–1568) stressed that love was a more powerful motivator for learning than fear (Ibid.:87); and

John Locke (1632–1704) believed that teaching could only be done in the spirit of love (Ibid.:123).

The philosopher Bertrand Russell (1926:185) also wrote about the importance of love in the early years of education. He considered love in education important enough to claim that 'all that has been done to improve the education of little children has been done by those who love them'. In the mid-twentieth century early years writers continued to make references to love. For example, de Lissa (1949) wrote about children's generosity in showing love to their teachers and of the need for this love to be reliably reciprocated. Gardner (1956) wrote that a child 'often shows very marked improvement, in many and often unexpected ways, once he is convinced that he is really loved and is able to give pleasure by his presence' (1956:19).

Gardner (1956:20) used the term 'loved people' to describe the adults who cared for very young children in nurseries. While she wrote that these 'loved people' were 'of less profound importance to a child's feelings' than their own parents, she also emphasised that children learn that they can share these loved people without losing their love.

Fletcher (1958:19) wrote about the importance of love between adults and children and stated that although it is not the same as love between parents and children, 'it is a love of children which is real, unchanging and very, very understanding'.

REFLECTION: LOVE IN EARLY YEARS SETTINGS

- What is your experience of loving children in your charge?

- What have parents said on the topic?

- How do you think love might support learning?

- What are some of the potential difficulties associated with love in out-of-home contexts?

There is evidence that by the 1960s, however, love in educational contexts was less widely encouraged. Winnicott (1964) wrote about the importance of love between a mother and a child and how this arose quite naturally. He said that parents knew how to care for their babies and children without thinking, and this was made possible through love. He also wrote that a teacher or a carer who is not a member of the family should adopt a very different role: 'She has, in contrast to the mother, technical knowledge derived from her training, and an attitude of objectivity towards the children under her care' (Winnicott, 1964:195).

Hence, despite repeated references to love in educational literature over the centuries, there was now a need to talk about relationships differently. Winnicott emphasised the more technical role of the professional teacher, as opposed to family members. A similar stance was adopted by Langford (1968:144) who wrote that practitioners' attitudes to children 'should reflect the necessarily temporary nature of their relationship', and that the word love itself has 'partiality built in'.

Many educationalists have highlighted ways in which love plays a significant role in education. However, since around the 1960s, this emphasis on love has lessened and other words and phrases have been used more widely: for example, care and attachment.

More recently, Page (2011) re-enlivened this focus on love. She found that parents wanted their children to be loved when in the care of other people. Manning-Morton and Thorp (2015) wrote that there are advantages for children when they know that they are loved by the people who care for them. Cousins (2015) found that practitioners constructed love as important in their work. The topic stimulated discussions about varied aspects of their practice, including teaching children lessons for the future, showing love through touch, relationships with parents, the extent to which they drew on their training or life experiences in relation to love, and allocation of work within teams according to people's natural propensity for love. Page (2015) later carried out research with a wider sample and developed a toolkit to support practitioners with this aspect of their work.

In Australia, White (2016) wrote about teaching with love. Children learn by the way they are touched and the loving sounds of those who communicate with them. From White's perspective, practitioners need to tune into children's diverse understandings of love, and love children in ways that children recognise as love. Love is re-emerging in professional discourses in early childhood education and care.

Training for love in early childhood

VIGNETTE: AN EARLY YEARS PRACTITIONER ON THE TOPIC OF LOVE

Anna: When I did my training it was very, like, you are not supposed to love children. You are supposed to just teach them, and, you know, keep your distance, not show any affection, not show any love. And I found that really difficult. I had it at the back of my mind while I was training because obviously I didn't want to fail and I thought, I can't, especially if I was being observed I knew not to do it. But once I qualified and I started working, it was like, actually, 'Who's to stop me?'

REFLECTION: TRAINING FOR LOVE

- How did your training prepare you to love children in your work?

- What are some of the issues, if any, that you face in relation to loving children in your work?

Why is attachment important in early years settings?

The concept of attachment is also associated with love. Attachment theory was developed by Bowlby in 1951 (Bowlby, 1988:24) out of a study about the effects of 'inadequate maternal care in early childhood'. It drew attention to the distress of children separated from their loved ones and suggested approaches to compensate or lessen the effects of this. Bowlby (1988:32) emphasised that children form 'enduring attachment[s] or attachment bond[s]' to very few people. This proximity, he argued, should be reliable and consistent, thereby enabling children to take risks, gradually moving away from their preferred individual. Bowlby (1988:40) said explicitly that he was writing about love; he described the formation of a bond between a child and an adult as 'falling in love', and the maintenance of such a bond as 'loving someone'.

Bowlby's attachment theory is still widely adopted today. Roberts' (2010:58) work on emotional well-being in young children, for example, stressed the importance of building strong attachments to enable children to develop 'loving and secure relationships'. Cortazar and Herreros' (2010) research about working with children with different attachment styles demonstrated the need for practitioners to strive to understand children's individual attachment histories. These researchers argued that child-centred approaches are not necessarily effective for all children, and some children in their research found it difficult to engage in play due to their particular attachment histories. As such, they proposed that practitioners attend to children's different attachment styles.

According to Read (2010:1), in her study about the importance of attachment in early years settings, practitioners should 'offer authentic love and care'. Attachments, for Read (2010:12), represent 'the unique relationship between a child and his primary caregiver that consists of numerous moment to moment interactions which foster future healthy development'.

Dowling (2014), too, emphasised the need for practitioners to form close attachments with children. For Dowling, 'The family ... has a powerful effect on each child's sense of identity, but when that child moves on to an early years setting the practitioners share this responsibility' (2014:91).

Elfer, Goldschmied and Selleck (2012:23) described the notion of attachment as being connected to another person by 'an elastic thread ... that allows for being apart as well as for being together'. When a child is well attached they can begin to take risks, explore their environments more confidently, communicate with others, develop independently. When the attachment is unavailable or unreliable, on the other hand, or there is no special person who will 'keep [the child] in mind' (Elfer et al., 2012:81), the child is likely to be less resilient or able to cope in times of stress.

The need for adults to be emotionally astute was emphasised by O'Connor (2013:13), especially in their role as 'secondary attachment figure[s]' for children. O'Connor stressed that children be 'warmly loved and cared for, responded to and valued unconditionally' in order to build up emotional resilience and feel 'worth loving' in return.

The studies mentioned above highlighted the importance of children establishing close attachments to particular adults, and that this would enhance children's future healthy emotional development. Some studies also pointed to the need for practitioners to be attentive to children's different attachment styles and to adapt their practice to match these. Attachment, from these perspectives, was understood as important for children's future healthy emotional development (Cousins, 2015).

The government (DfES, 2007), too, recognised the importance of attachments and stated that children benefit from developing strong relationships with one identified adult or 'key person' in the setting context. This 'key person' approach is still applied in the current statutory framework for the early years foundation stage (DfE, 2017:22–23).

NOTION OF KEY PERSON ENSHRINED IN POLICY IN ENGLAND

3.27. Each child must be assigned a key person. Their role is to help ensure that every child's care is tailored to meet their individual needs ... to help the child become familiar with the setting, offer a settled relationship for the child and build a relationship with their parents.

This key person approach offers 'real daily meaning and emotional significance' (Elfer et al., 2012:24) for children and their families, and, as Elfer et al. (2012) proposed, allows children to feel special, cherished and carefully attended to, even when they are away from home.

Different sorts of attachments in early years settings?

As discussed in the introduction, some authors have argued that it is inappropriate to develop attachments in non-familial, public contexts (Dencik, 1989; Dahlberg, Moss and Pence, 2007; Degotardi and Pearson, 2009). These authors suggest, instead, that institutional settings offer a qualitatively different experience to that offered in familial, private contexts. In public contexts, they argue, children build different sorts of relationships with the many adults who care for them, and with the numerous peers they interact with. In settings, children are able to form multiple attachments, and experience many different sorts of relationships.

So, on the one hand, some authors write about the importance of attachments in early years settings, and, on the other hand, different authors write about the distinct experiences and quality of relationships that are afforded in non-familial contexts. Both positions are important. Young children benefit from experiencing close attachments to significant adults in non-familial contexts, and, on the other hand, what they experience and learn in these contexts is qualitatively different.

We believe that attachments are wholly appropriate in non-familial, public contexts. Brain research teaches us that children's brains develop within relationships with sensitive, significant others. Indeed, as Lebedeva (2015) points out, all learning takes place within relationships. Well-trained professionals can act on their knowledge and understanding of this area of brain and social sciences in order to build close relationships with individual children and their families, respond appropriately to different behaviours, form attachments with children, and support children to make the most of their early childhood.

REFLECTION: LOVE IN EARLY YEARS SETTINGS

■ What is your experience of loving children in your charge?

■ What have parents said on the topic?

■ How do you think love might support learning?

■ What are some of the potential difficulties associated with love in out-of-home contexts?

Support for practitioners who work with emotions

There is a need, as proposed by Page and Elfer (2013), to acknowledge the complexity of work in early childhood. It is possible that some practitioners, for example, may form attachments with some children, feel a sense of loss when children leave their care, be unable to talk freely about affective matters in the workplace, or be worried about touching children as a sign of love (Cousins, 2015).

One form of support is to provide opportunities for practitioners to reflect on their own practice. Manning-Morton (2006:48) advocated this in a study of quality provision for birth to three-year-olds. She emphasised the importance of practitioners developing as mature, emotionally intelligent, self-aware adults, and 'becom[ing] experts in themselves'. She suggested that practitioners are given high levels of support so that they can more successfully meet the day-to-day challenges, for example, rejection by children. She also highlighted that work with very young children involves practitioners' hearts as much as their minds.

Similarly, Osgood (2011:131) argued that practitioners need 'improved support' for this work. She suggested this from the point of view of mitigating the human cost of this 'emotionally demanding work'. Osgood (2011:130) proposed that if early years practitioners were allowed to draw on their 'life experience and wisdom', as indicated within her concept of 'professionalism from within', they might develop an even 'deeper-level appreciation for the work (i.e. professionalism)'. The complexity of the role was also emphasised by Harwood et al. (2013) who proposed that more opportunities be established for participants to talk about the emotional aspects of their roles.

Page and Elfer (2013:564) noted that staff often adopted 'a largely intuitive approach' in their daily work, 'drawing on personal experience rather than a body of theoretical knowledge'. They advocated that managers should offer opportunities for staff to talk about difficult aspects of their work, and allow any issues to be openly discussed. As such, they recommended that managers should promote a climate whereby individuals feel comfortable in raising questions and problems and accept that there may be no clear answers. Practitioners should be able to express their feelings and worries in a non-judgemental atmosphere. Page and Elfer pointed to the need for appropriate support for these complex matters associated with love.

VIGNETTE: PRACTITIONERS PLAY A TEMPORARY, RATHER THAN CONSTANT, ROLE

How does Maimoonah, room manager at a large workplace nursery, manage situations when children show affection to her when their parents come to collect them at the end of the day?

The foundation of our relationship with a child is built through their parents, so as a practitioner I feel it is important to acknowledge their feelings. Many parents are taken aback and will seem hurt when their child comes towards me at pick-up time. I try to reassure the parent that their child is playing a game and looking for attention. I feel it is important to put the feelings of the parent first as they will always be a constant in their child's life, whereas as a practitioner I am only a temporary.

■ Why do you think some children go to her when their parents pick them up?

■ How does Maimoonah manage these situations?

This emphasis on the need for reflective talk was applied in research by Goouch and Powell (2013:81–82) who set up a project for baby room practitioners. This was in response to practitioners' stated need for 'specific development opportunities', and their sense of feeling 'poorly supported' in their work with babies. Goouch and Powell found that the baby room practitioners were very willing to engage in the project and learn from each other. Goouch and Powell (2013:83) found that these 'critical spaces' for talking and thinking helped the practitioners 'to develop a sense of their own worth in their work and to develop a "voice"' (2013:87). The researchers found that creating times for talk helped practitioners to reflect on their practice and gain a deeper understanding about aspects of their work. This research was significant because it emphasised the importance of 'professional talk' (2013:83) in the context of people's work in early years. These opportunities for talk, according to Goouch and Powell, helped the practitioners in their research to understand their experiences in the baby room at a deeper level, value their work, make connections with their own life experiences, and consider other possibilities. Goouch and Powell found that talk was a powerful learning experience for early years practitioners.

The complexity of the role of early years practitioners, then, is widely written about, as is the importance of loving children in early years contexts. However, authors agree that this carries challenges, often unspoken and unacknowledged. Page (2010, 2011) found that there was a need for a professional language of love to be developed through which to explore this complex work. Osgood (2011) called for more space to be made for people to draw on their subjective experiences to enhance their professional practice. Goouch and Powell (2013) emphasised the value of talk.

Healthy emotional climates in early years settings

Howes (2011:257) noted that the 'emotional climate' in early years settings can support or impede children's development. Settings with positive emotional climates are pleasant places to be in. They are places where adults and children communicate well, laugh together and express a sense of enjoyment as they engage in different activities and interactions with each other. In these emotionally healthy climates, practitioners are themselves also emotionally well, or 'emotionally literate' (Weare, 2015:11).

The emotions of children and practitioners are present in all situations with young children. It is therefore important for practitioners to be aware of their own moods when joining in with children in their play or supporting them through difficult moments (Ouvry, 2015). Such self-aware practitioners are warm and sensitive to all of the children, and become fully involved in what the children do. They do not get angry with the children or become bored in any sense. They establish clear routines and guidelines, and children thrive within these 'cultural markers' (Howes, 2011:257).

Children in settings with positive emotional climates are likely to develop positive relationships with the adults who care for them. A positive emotional climate also facilitates positive peer relationships. Children learn to share their spaces with other children, consider the needs of others and develop friendly dispositions.

The physical environment of early years settings, including home settings, can support emotional education. Moss (2010:15) emphasised the holistic aspect of early years education whereby 'caring (for self, others and the environment) and learning, health and upbringing are viewed as inseparable conditions for flourishing'. Babies and very young children need to feel safe, at home and loved in their environment. Open learning spaces and home-like centres, which, as Hedges (2010:36) recommended, are not 'separated from everyday worlds of families and communities' can contribute to children's emotional development. The practice of separating children from the wider community and environment, then, may not always be the best way to support healthy emotional development.

In Denmark many nurseries are established with home-like features. In these purpose-built centres, the kitchen is often positioned at the heart of the learning environment, with the children. This design is based on an understanding about

Figure 3.1 The kitchen at the heart of Preschool Trehoje, Denmark, Photograph by Sarah Cousins (2007).

the importance of children learning to care for themselves, others and the environment. Anning (2006:5) highlighted, in particular, 'the calm informality and physical freedom' experienced by young Danish children. In such open-plan centres children can participate in healthy food preparation, talk to the cook, feel part of the community, experience closeness with adults over a continuous period, build trust and learn first-hand about love. In home-like settings such as these children are more likely to experience 'consistency in their relationships with their adult carers' (Nutbrown, 2011:38) and have the opportunity to flourish.

REFLECTION: ESTABLISHING HOMELY SETTINGS

- How do you help children to feel at home in your setting?

- How do you organise your environment to support a comfortable atmosphere?

- What do practitioners at your setting do to help children feel cherished, experience love and grow in self-esteem?

Conclusion

In this chapter the meaning of emotional learning was explored. Strong synergies were found between notions of love, attachment and emotion. The complexities of working with emotions and supporting children's emotional development were emphasised. The importance of developing positive emotional climates in settings with 'emotionally literate' (Weare, 2015:11) adults was discussed. The next chapter considers the meaning of sensory learning, and how this works alongside children's emotional development.

References

Anning, A. (2006) *Promoting Children's Learning from Birth to Five: Developing the New Early Years Professional*, 2nd edition. Buckingham: Open University Press.

Bos, K., Zeanah, C.H., Fox, N.A., Drury, S.S., McLaughlin, K.A. & Nelson, C.A. (2011) Psychiatric outcomes in young children with a history of institutionalization. *Harvard Review Psychiatry*, 19 (1), 15–24.

Bowlby, J. (1988) *A Secure Base: Clinical Applications of Attachment Theory*. Abingdon: Routledge.

Children's Society, The (2015) *The Children's Society Report 2015*. Online at: www.childrenssociety.org.uk

Cortazar, A. & Herreros, F. (2010) Early attachment relationships and the early childhood curriculum. *Contemporary Issues in Early Childhood*, 11 (2), 192–202.

Cousins, S. (2015) *Practitioners' Constructions of Love in the Context of Early Childhood Education and Care: A Narrative Inquiry* (Unpublished EdD research thesis, University of Sheffield, Sheffield). Online at: http://etheses.whiterose.ac.uk/8855/

Dahlberg, G., Moss, P. & Pence, A. (2007) *Beyond Quality in Early Childhood Education and Care: Languages of Evaluation*, 2nd edition. London: Routledge.

Degotardi, S. & Pearson, E. (2009) Relationship theory in the nursery: Attachment and beyond. *Contemporary Issues in Early Childhood*, 10 (2), 144–155.

de Lissa, L. (1949) *Life in the Nursery School and in Early Babyhood*. London: Longman, Green and Co Ltd.

Dencik, L. (1989) Growing up in a post-modern age: On the child's situation in the modern family, and on the position of the family in the modern welfare state. *Acta Sociologica*, 32 (2), 155–180.

Department for Education (DfE) (2017) *Statutory framework for the early years foundation stage*. Online at: www.gov.uk/government/publications

Department for Education and Department of Health (2015) *Special Educational Needs and Disability Code of Practice: 0–25 Years*. Available at: www.gov.uk/government/publications

Department for Education and Skills (DfES) (2007) *Early Years Foundation Stage: Setting the Standards for Learning, Development and Care for Children from Birth to Five*. London: DfES/Sure Start.

Dowling, M. (2010) Strength of Feeling. *Nursery World* (Haymarket Business Publications Ltd). 3/11/2010, 110 (4210), p. 14–16. Online at: www.nurseryworld.co.uk

Dowling, M. (2014) *Young Children's Personal, Social and Emotional Development*, 4th edition. London: Sage.

Elfer, P., Goldschmied, E. & Selleck, D.Y. (2012). *Key persons in the Early Years: Building Relationships for Quality Provision in Early Years Settings and Primary Schools*, 2nd edition. Abingdon: Routledge.

Fletcher, M.I. (1958) *The Adult and the Nursery School Child*. Toronto, Canada. University of Toronto Press.

Gardner, D.E.M. (1956) *The Education of Young Children*. London: Methuen.

Goouch, K. & Powell, S. (2013) Orchestrating professional development for baby room practitioners: Raising the stakes in new dialogic encounters. *Journal of Early Childhood Research*, 11 (1), 78–92. DOI: http://dx.doi.org/10.1177/1476718X12448374

Harwood, D., Klopper, A., Osanyin, A. & Vanderlee, M. (2013) 'It's more than care': Early childhood educators' concepts of professionalism. *Early Years: An International Research Journal*, 33 (1), 4–17.

Hedges, H., (2010) Whose goals and interests? The interface of children's play and teachers' pedagogical practices. In L. Brooker & S. Edwards (eds), *Engaging Play*. (pp. 25–38) Berkshire, Open University Press.

Howes, C. (2011) Children's social development within the socialisation context of child care and early childhood education. In P.K. Smith & C. H. Hart (eds), *The Wiley-Blackwell Handbook of Child Social Development*, 2nd edition (pp. 246–262). Chichester: Wiley-Blackwell.

Janks, H. (2010) *Literacy and Power*. New York: Routledge.

Langford, G. (1968) *Philosophy and Education: An Introduction*. Basingstoke: Macmillan Education Ltd.

Lawrence, E. (1970) *The Origins and Growth of Modern Education*. Harmondsworth: Penguin Books.

Lebedeva, G. (2015) Building brains one relationship at a time. *Exchange*, 11, Nov/Dec 2015, 21–25.

Madrid, S., Fernie, D. & Kantor, R. (2014) *Reframing the Emotional Worlds of the Early Childhood Classroom*. New York: Routledge.

Manning-Morton, J. (2006) The personal is professional: Professionalism and the birth to threes practitioner. *Contemporary Issues in Early Childhood*, 7 (1), 42–52.

Manning-Morton, J. & Thorp, M. (2015) *Two-year-olds in Early Years Settings: Journeys of Discovery*. Maidenhead: Open University Press.

Moss, P. (2010) We cannot continue as we are: The educator in an education for survival. *Contemporary Issues in Early Childhood*, 11(1), 8–19.

Nutbrown, C. (2011) *Threads of Thinking: Schemas and Young Children's Learning*, 4th edition. London: Sage Publications.

O'Connor, A. (2013) Love, attachments and transitions. *The Journal of the British Association for Early Childhood Education*, 70, Summer 2013. London: Early Education.

Osgood, J. (2011) Contested constructions of professionalism within the nursery. In L. Miller & C. Cable (eds), *Professionalization, Leadership and Management in the Early Years* (pp. 107–118). London: Sage Publications.

Ouvry, M. (2015) *Going Out to Play and Learn*. Learning together series. London: Early Education. Online at: https://www.early-education.org.uk/sites/default/files/Going%20out%20to%20play%20and%20learn%20%283%29.pdf

Page, J. (2010) *Mothers, Work and Childcare: Choices, Beliefs and Dilemmas*. Volumes 1 and 2. (Unpublished PhD research thesis, University of Sheffield, Sheffield). Retrieved from http://ethos.bl.uk

Page, J. (2011) Do mothers want professional carers to love their babies? *Journal of Early Childhood Research*, 1 (14), 1–14.

Page, J. (2015) *Professional Love in Early Years Settings (PLEYS), Attachment toolkit. Booklet 2*. University of Sheffield.

Page, J. & Elfer, P. (2013) The emotional complexity of attachment interactions in nursery. *European Early Childhood Education Research Journal*, 21 (4), 553–567.

Piper, H. & Smith, H. (2003) 'Touch' in educational and child care settings: Dilemmas and responses. *British Educational Research Journal*. 29 (6), 879–894.

Read, V. (2010) *Developing Attachment in Early Years Settings*. Abingdon: David Fulton.

Roberts, H. (2015) *Playtime: An evidence-informed scoping review on children's play with a focus on older children and middle childhood*. University of Cambridge: Centre for Science and Policy.

Roberts, R. (2010) *Wellbeing from Birth*. London: Sage Publications.

Robinson, M. & May, P. (2014) *The Feeling Child: Laying the Foundation for Confidence and Resilience*. London: David Fulton.

Russell, B. (1926) *On Education Especially in Early Childhood*. London: George Allen and Unwin Ltd.

Weare, K. (2015) *What Works in Promoting Social and Emotional Well-Being and Responding to Mental Health Problems in Schools? Advice for schools and framework document*. London: National Children's Bureau. Online at: https://www.mentalhealth.org.nz/assets/ResourceFinder/What-works-in-promoting-social-and-emotional-wellbeing-in-schools-2015.pdf

Weaver, M. (2014) 'Jimmy Savile gave Rolf Harris guided tour of Broadmoor', The Guardian Newspaper, 1 July 2014. Online at: https://www.theguardian.com/media/2014/jul/01/jimmy-savile-rolf-harris-alleged-tour-broadmoor

White, E.J. (2016) *Introducing Dialogic Pedagogy: Provocations for the Early Years*. London: Routledge.

Wilson, R. & Wilson, R.L. (2015) *Understanding Emotional Development: Providing Insight into Human Lives*. London: Routledge.

Winicott, D.W. (1964) *The Child, the Family, and the Outside World*. Harmondsworth: Penguin Books.

4 Sensory learning

OVERVIEW OF THE CHAPTER

This chapter is about sensory learning in early childhood contexts. It explores:

- How we understand 'the senses'

- Why sensory learning is important

- Theories related to sensory learning

- The value of sensory learning in child development, with reference to particular examples, including learning outdoors and learning through music

- Issues and tensions related to sensory learning with specific reference to inclusion and children with SEND

Introduction

This chapter focuses on learning through the senses. In the previous chapter, we noted that children develop an emotional blueprint made up of associations between their physical and sensory experiences and feelings (Janks, 2010). This chapter explores key questions and issues around these sensory experiences and sensory learning in the early years. What is sensory learning? Why is sensory learning important? How can sensory learning contribute to child development? Is the outdoor environment a useful arena for sensory learning? Can musical experiences enhance learning? What challenges emerge for early years practitioners when implementing sensory learning in practice? How can early years practitioners be adequately prepared to do this work?

What is sensory learning?

It has traditionally been believed that humans have five senses, that is, touch, sight, hearing, smell and taste. In the last seventy years another sense known as proprioception has emerged. This sense is 'the ability to recognise and use the physical sensations from the body that give feedback on balance and the position of our limbs' (Lindon, 2005:121). So proprioception enables an awareness of the body's position and movement in space – some have called it kinaesthesia (Pound, 2009). Blythe (2004, in Lindon, 2005) related proprioception to an understanding of the body's messages in relation to touch, grasp and balance. Some have extended this to include somatic senses which enable us to map our peripersonal space so that our brains map the space we move in and any tools we use in that space (Blakeslee and Blakeslee, 2007). For example, when children use a pencil or paintbrush their sense of peripersonal space extends to the end of the writing tool that they are using. Likewise, if they are playing a game using a bat their sense of peripersonal space extends to the end of the bat that they are playing with. Similarly, a child who is drawing with a water responsive mat may become aware, not only of the drawing tools they are using like stamps, brushes and pens, but also of sitting on one of their artistic creations. For example, having drawn 'daddy pig' a child may become aware of sitting on daddy pig and even squashing daddy pig. Blakeslee and Blakeslee refer to touch and proprioception, thermoception (sense of heat and cold), nocioception (sense of pain) and equilibrioception (sense of balance) (Pound, 2009:66). Therefore, early childhood experiences or play which engage any of the above senses can be regarded as sensory play and such play or experience which stimulates the neural pathways of the brain is a vital element in children's early brain development and a fundamental basis for learning skills.

Having explored how we understand the senses, it is important to think about sensory learning and the reasons why such learning is considered vital in early years education.

Why is it important to focus on the senses?

In the first two years of life, children learn mainly through exploring the world through their senses (Santer, Griffiths with Goodall, 2007). This type of physical discovery is crucial to help children comprehend the world.

> Exploration is essential if we are to build up in the brain a representation or 'model' which is useful for the accurate interpretation of the world ... building up knowledge of the world through our senses and by trial and error is the basis of all later intellectual activity.
>
> (Brierley, 1994:75–76)

As such, children explore the world using their senses, absorbing a range of experiences, and the quality of these experiences has an impact on their brain development. Other research around the development of the brain suggests that children's experiences in the early years have an impact on the biological structure of the brain and learning ability, and that a dearth of such early experiences may result in a profound reduction in the brain's potential (Griffiths, 2003; Brown and Jernigan, 2012; Lebedeva, 2015). However, it is necessary to be aware of the fact that neuroscience is in its infancy and Tomlinson (2017:115) has raised concerns about 'brain-based' approaches to teaching being based on inaccurate links with neuroscience.

According to Piaget (1971) the sensori-motor stage of learning is a stage that takes place during the first two years of a child's life. During this stage they learn through physical action and their senses. After this they enter the pre-operational stage before going through the concrete operational then formal operational stages of learning. Piaget did not adopt a flexible approach to these stages. In other words, once a child has left the sensori-motor stage aged two years there will be no return to it. The implications are that once the opportunity for sensori-motor learning has passed after two years of age the opportunity for brain development through sensori-motor learning has been lost or reduced. Piaget's theory has been challenged because of its inflexibility and because it does not recognise the unpredictable nature of learning (Santer et al., 2007). Bruner (1960), however, while maintaining that physical action characterises early learning, viewed this as an 'enactive' or initial stage of learning which is employed every time we encounter a new experience. From this perspective, the opportunity for brain development through sensory learning is not lost after the age of two years. Gardner identified six or eight bodily intelligences in his theory of multiple intelligences (1983). For Gardner, bodily kinaesthetic intelligence was one of these intelligences and involved physical expression of ideas. Gardner argued that there is a 'relationship between the mental and physical, the reflective and the active' (Pound, 2008:64).

Clearly, whichever theory is adopted in relation to sensory learning, every child needs to explore and learn through all their senses. This is especially important since 'in the foundation years children are laying pathways in the brain which will be the foundation of all future learning' (Pound, 2009:66).

> Neuroscientists refer to the notion that experience changes brains by strengthening the relevant connections and eliminating the irrelevant ones; in other words, the brain is customized according to its experiences ('neurons that fire together wire together'). This is the basis for the highly efficient learning in the first three years when neural organization rate is at its peak: a lack of stimulation will prevent and prune connections, and high stimulation will make connections stronger.
>
> (Lebedeva, 2015:23)

The importance of sensory learning is also clearly reflected in current government guidance for learning in the early years in England. The Early Years Foundation Stage Profile 2017 handbook states that:

> Finding out and exploring is concerned with the child's open-ended hands-on experiences which result from innate curiosity. These experiences provide raw sensory material from which the child builds concepts, tests ideas and finds out.
>
> (Standards and Testing Agency (STA), 2016:23)

One of the Early Learning Goals focuses on 'understanding of the world' which involves helping children to make sense of the physical world by affording them opportunities for exploration and discovering the environment. As such they will be able to:

> ...know about similarities and differences in relation to places, objects, materials and living things. They talk about the features of their own immediate environment and how environments might vary from one another. They make observations of animals and plants and explain why some things occur, and talk about changes.
>
> (STA, 2016:30)

Similarly, the Early Learning Goal which focuses on 'expressive arts and design' focuses on supporting children to explore a wide range of media and materials and giving them opportunities to express their ideas through art, music, movement, dance, role play, and design and technology. Early Learning Goal 16 involves children singing, making music and dancing. It also focuses on investigating a wide range of materials, colour, design, texture, form and function. Children need to have their own first-hand experiences of these materials in order to fully understand them, so the importance of sensory learning in the early years is clearly evident in the current Early Learning Goals in England.

REFLECTION: SENSORY LEARNING

- Identify experiences or aspects of play in the early years that enhance the sense of touch, sight, hearing, taste and smell

- How do these experiences relate to the Early Learning Goals?

- How helpful or realistic is it to include experiences related to Blakeslee and Blakeslee's (2007) additional senses?

This section has introduced the importance of sensory learning. The following section explores this in more detail, focusing on how sensory learning has a positive impact on specific aspects of child development and learning in the early years.

How does sensory learning affect development in the early years?

When children are engaged in sensory experiences they learn. As such, stimulation of the senses through movement and sensory experiences is an essential contributor to brain development in the early years (Pound, 2008, 2009; Brown and Jernigan, 2012; Lebedeva, 2015). Thus, few researchers would disagree with the importance of sensory experiences, including movement activities, in the early years in order to maximise brain development. Chugani (1998) advocated 'windows of opportunity', or times when certain sensory experiences have the most impact on child development. However, he maintained that missing these hypothetical 'windows of opportunity' may result in children not developing to their full potential. It is important to note, however, that he did not envisage the gap, or 'window', closing, but only narrowing.

Sensory learning has an impact on many aspects of early childhood development, including physical, cognitive, language, communication, social, emotional and creative skills. Physical skills are developed as muscles work together to develop fine and gross motor skills. Gross motor skills involve using large bodily muscles and are associated with activities like running, jumping, throwing, catching, climbing stairs and walking. When children explore different surfaces, like grass and tarmac, lift different objects or throw a ball or Frisbee, they develop these gross motor skills. Fine motor skills involve the coordination of muscle movements which are needed in everyday life, like picking up small objects, using a knife and fork, opening and closing zips, tying and untying shoelaces, fastening buttons. These fine motor skills enable children to become independent, for example, in eating and dressing themselves. Fine motor skills are also essential in controlling pencils, pens and paint brushes. Accordingly, they are a vital precursor to developing writing skills. Furthermore, children use fine motor skills to turn the pages of a book, so need these skills to develop as independent readers, or to play a musical instrument, for example. Brierley (1994:26) in Santer et al. (2007) concluded that 'The activity of the motor system is initiated and controlled through its sensory connections. During the Early Years children explore constantly and their activities develop gross and fine motor control'.

Sensory learning not only develops physical skills, but it also enhances cognitive development so that young children use their senses to understand and learn about new things. For example, touching something smooth and then something rough or a wet object and then a similar object when dry helps children to understand different surfaces and the characteristics of those surfaces. So, the sensation of touch supports brain development in the area of sorting and classifying. Goldschmied and Jackson (1994) suggested using a 'treasure basket' containing a range of natural objects like pine cones, shells and ordinary household objects for children aged 6–9 months to explore through their senses. In feeling these natural objects, young children make decisions about what they prefer to feel and touch, so begin making choices about what they like. They may begin to feel pleasure from their favourite objects and preferred surfaces. They also develop hand–eye coordination as they take an object out of the treasure basket and move it towards their mouth. Once children reach the age of 12–20 months they extend their understanding, ascribing names to objects, learning to store objects away in bags, becoming familiar with the routines of storage and aware that they must take turns to put objects away. This kind of sensory learning takes place before the more complex understanding in mathematics and science (Siraj-Blatchford and Siraj-Blatchford, 2002). For example, young children may feel the difference between warm water, ice and snow and even decide which they prefer to touch and feel before they begin to understand the scientific explanations of why water can take different forms in different temperatures. Similarly, young children will feel the two-ness of two as they hold two dry limes in their hands. Children learn in sensory ways.

These sensory experiences support children's problem solving and decision making. Children become amateur scientists predicting, observing and developing analytical skills. Scientific skills can be developed, for example, through understanding how to make icing in different colours for cup-cakes or how to make substances like sand or flour stick together by adding water. Similarly, mathematical skills of matching, sorting and counting are developed when children feel, observe and match objects of different sizes and shapes. Musical skills are developed as children experiment with different materials to make different sounds, for example crumpling and tearing paper, ringing bells or banging two objects together.

Sensory experiences can also contribute to social and emotional development. As children experience different tastes, feelings, sights, sounds and smells they learn what they like and dislike and how to convey these preferences to others. This in turn helps them to make their own choices about what they want to eat, the programmes and music they want to listen to, or what they want to wear. Some children select a favourite blanket or soft toy which feels pleasant to the touch and provides emotional comfort. As such, expressing preferences to adults and children around them enables children to communicate and interact, thus developing a sense of themselves and an understanding of other children's preferences and dislikes. Such understandings enhance the relationships children have with parents, teachers and peers as they learn to collaborate and communicate. For example, children begin expressing a preference to watch a particular television programme, or look at a favourite book, rather than any other. In time they may articulate the specific episodes of the programme or sections of the book they prefer.

Finally, sensory learning can contribute to children's development in literacy. As children experience a range of likes and dislikes, they learn to communicate these to others, thus developing their descriptive and expressive language skills. For example, they learn new words to describe objects and experiences like 'rough' for a tree bark, 'smooth' for a plastic ball, 'wet' or 'smelly' for leaves, and 'soft' or 'squidgy' for mud. Some descriptive words like 'squidgy' or 'slimy' mean nothing to children until they have felt the wet mud, or similar substances. It is difficult to explain a situation of losing your balance until you have experienced standing on a 'wobbly' stone, riding on a balance bicycle or walking along a narrow ridge. Using such descriptive and expressive language encourages creativity and the ability to tell and write stories and engage in role play. As stated earlier, children also develop gross and fine motor skills through sensori-motor activities which enhance writing skills.

REFLECTION: DEVELOPING SKILLS THROUGH SENSORY LEARNING

■ Consider examples of sensory experiences in the early years that enhance problem-solving skills, e.g. what is safe to touch and what is dangerous

■ Reflect on the ways in which sensory experiences enhance the skill of classifying and sorting

■ Consider how such skills may contribute to emotional and social development

---

Having explored some of the benefits of sensory experiences and their contribution to aspects of children's learning in the early years, it is clear that children will need help to explore with their senses and to experience a range of textures, sounds, sights, smells and tastes. Some specific examples of the contribution to learning and development in the early years that a variety of sensory experiences make will now be considered, including learning through the outdoor environment and learning through musical experiences.

Sensory learning outdoors

Bilton (2002) viewed being outdoors as one of the most powerful ways in which young children can learn. Maynard and Waters (2007) highlighted that a renewed interest in learning outdoors has been evident in the development of the Forest School Approach (Waite, Davies and Brown, 2006) and the fresh interest in the development of school grounds (McKendrick, 2005). Forest Schools initially outlined their principles in 2002, focusing on the long-term planning of outdoor activities rather than one-off outdoor activities. The schools support the relationship of the learner with the natural world so lessons take place in woodland or natural environments. The aim is to enhance independence, risk-taking, confidence and creativity.

Research has identified many advantages of learning outdoors. Children can make noise and mess much more readily than they can indoors (Bilton, 2002; Ouvry, 2003). Tovey (2007) also mentioned benefits in the freedom and excitement of the outdoors which is an acceptable environment for feeling a sense of glee and abandonment. There are many natural items outdoors that cannot be found indoors which can 'excite curiosity, exploration and wonder' (Pound, 2009:76). For example, experiences such as jumping in muddy puddles or wading through leaves are available exclusively in outdoor contexts. Experiencing the sights, smells and sounds of a farmyard animal, milking a goat or stroking a large animal are sensory experiences that children can only find outdoors.

Gardner identified the importance of naturalistic intelligence and Richard Louv (2010) suggested that children need to be protected from 'nature deficit disorder', where they are denied such opportunities to explore and play outdoors. He identified naturalistic intelligence as the eighth intelligence, emphasising the wide range of learning that emanates from the natural environment so that nature is a totally sensory experience for children. Tovey (2007:66) similarly articulates the benefits of large spaces outdoors which offer children the opportunity to use the sense of proprioception and 'know their place in space', thus developing spatial awareness.

The sensory experiences of excitement and freedom can enhance emotional and physical health by promoting a sense of well-being and contribute to mental health. Santer et al. (2007:47) viewed play as a 'form of catharsis' and a means to maintaining emotional balance and mental health. They cited Street (2002:1) who stated that play 'fosters resilience to stressful life events'. Research done in Scandinavia has shown that children who play outdoors in natural environments are healthier and have better fitness, balance and coordination than children who do not (Fjortoft, 2001, 2004, in Maynard and Waters, 2007).

VIGNETTE: AN INTERNATIONAL APPROACH

At a nursery in Denmark, children take the lead in their learning outdoors. Pedagogues (practitioners) follow them through the fields and woods, and are there in the moment as they discover an insect, gasp in awe or express themselves in words. These highly skilled and attuned pedagogues listen and watch their children. They repeat what they say with any new vocabulary, offer challenges, witness their learning, show an interest or reveal their pride. Children feel safe to explore their environment. They know the extent of the area they can traverse, and are sure that the adults who care for them are constant. Children go back to the hut to read by the fire, have lunch or rest.

■ How do the nursery pedagogues in Denmark encourage independence, risk-taking, confidence and creativity in the children?

■ How do they provide opportunities for children to experience freedom and feel excited about their learning?

Learning outdoors develops self-confidence and a willingness to take risks (Stephenson, 2003; Pound, 2009). Risk-taking and making decisions about what is safe and what is not, also provide children with a sense of agency in making their own decisions. Such outdoor learning can also be used to foster awareness of the natural world and encourage positive attitudes to preserving the natural environment. It can develop life-skills, for example, learning how to grow vegetables, the need to water gardens and plants and remove weeds or the ability to decipher edible from non-edible plants.

REFLECTION: OUTDOOR LEARNING

■ In what ways does the natural environment enhance emotional well-being and mental health?

■ Reflect on an outdoor sensory play activity that enhanced a child's sense of risk-taking and self-confidence

■ What specific sensory experiences in the outdoors could you use to encourage positive attitudes to the natural world in children?

This section explored some of the benefits related to sensory learning in natural and outdoor environments. The next section explores the potential benefits of musical experiences and their contribution to learning in the early years.

Learning through music and sound

The sensory experience of listening to music and expressing oneself musically through song, rhythm, beat and musical instruments is one that can bring much pleasure. However, the benefits of music and sound are widely recognised to go beyond enjoyment. Music has much value in enhancing children's development in a wide range of skills, particularly mathematics and literacy. Howard Gardner (1983) included 'musical intelligence' as one of the intelligences in his theory of multiple intelligences and considered musical intelligence as one of the earliest intelligences to emerge (Pound, 2008:64). The importance of acquiring the skills of literacy and mathematical skills in England are clearly reflected in the curriculum and essential requirements for professional jobs and academic courses. It is important, however, that children enjoy a range of sensory, playful experiences on their way. These pleasurable experiences can lead children to understand new mathematical concepts or express themselves through language. Sensory experiences can form the basis of literacy and mathematical skills in the early years and are therefore an essential foundation for learning for the future.

Mathematics and music are associated in the brain from early in a child's life (Burack, 2005). Very young children have the capacity to respond to music and the mathematical concepts evident in music. It is particularly important to use music to support the development of mathematical concepts in the early years, especially with children aged from 0–5 years old (Linder, Powers-Costello and Stegelin, 2011, cited in Geist, Geist and Kuznik, 2012:74). Young children not only see patterns, but hear them in music, so using music to enhance these patterns may contribute to the development of cognitive skills. For example, when singing songs like 'Five little ducks' they learn counting skills like addition and subtraction. Another simple example of using music to enhance mathematical skills is the song 'One potato, two potatoes'. Children can enjoy this song, learning to count from one to ten. They can also learn to stack the potatoes by using their fists, moving their hands from the bottom to the top of the potato pile. The activity can be inclusive, ensuring all children in the group have a chance to put their fist (potato) in the pile, also encouraging teamwork and turn-taking. When children perform these actions and sing these songs with enjoyment, on a regular basis and with familiar adults who care for them, then the learning opportunities are rich.

As such, children begin learning mathematical skills early in life and these mathematical skills develop when the young child is actively participating in everyday, real-life situations and contexts (Geist et al., 2012). Above all, music is a pleasurable activity and if children associate learning mathematical skills with enjoyment they are more likely to engage in mathematics learning.

Music not only enhances children's mathematical skills, but it also contributes to literacy development. In recent years, there has been an increased emphasis on the importance of rhyme and rhythm and how these contribute to language development (Adams et al., 2002). Many similarities are evident between music and literacy and therefore music is essential in ensuring literacy development. Children use auditory skills to develop phoneme awareness, learning to discriminate between different sounds and putting sounds together to form words. Musical skills are related to auditory discrimination which is essential for phonological awareness and reading skills. Children who have musical experiences develop the aural skills needed for spoken sounds more quickly than those who do not have those experiences (Gromko, 2005; Anvari et al., 2002, in Chau and Riforgiate, 2010). Also, people use variation in pitch, volume, tone and rhythm in conversation and verbal communication in the same way as music uses different volume, keys and pitch. Even limited musical experiences enhance pitch and rhythm discrimination in speech (Hyde et al., 2009; Moreno et al., 2009, in Chau and Riforgiate, 2010).

The 'Animal Hand-Clap Rap' (Buchanan, 2012) is an excellent example of an enjoyable song that can be used to teach phoneme awareness. The song also enhances animal vocabulary and uses clapping to reinforce the sounds.

Animal Hand-Clap Rap

Do the hand-clapping rap, do the hand-clapping rap, yeah, yeah
Do the hand-clapping rap, do the hand-clapping rap, yeah, yeah

Let's get started, clap the fun, clapping animals, start with one:
deer frog owl dog
bear goose bat moose
You've got it down, here's what we'll do, clap more creatures! Make it two:
tiger panda otter squirrel
rabbit eagle lion turtle

Chorus

You're doing great, so clap with me, so many great animals. Make it three:
pelican butterfly octopus cockatoo
elephant rattlesnake crocodile kangaroo

We can't stop now, let's clap some more awesome creatures. Make it four:
rhinoceros alligator tarantula caterpillar
armadillo dromedary orangutan salamander

Importantly, the song is an opportunity for children to feel safe and cared for by the people who sing it with them. Music is a communal act.

Many songs for children develop rhyming skills, an essential aspect of literacy development; for example, 'Hickory Dickory Dock' and 'Baa Baa Black Sheep'. As children sing and chant songs and rhymes they develop oral language, phonological awareness, vocabulary and thinking skills which are essential elements of literacy.

> Music is an integral part of a quality early childhood curriculum. It plays a role in setting the tone of the classroom, developing skills and concepts, helping children make transitions, and building a sense of community. Of course, if you ask the children, they will tell you singing is a fun part of their daily activities.
>
> (Schiller, 2008:1)

Literacy is more than reading, writing and comprehension, it is a social act which involves listening and speaking. Vygotsky's Social Development Theory emphasises the necessity of social interaction in child development (Tarbert,

2012). In singing, chanting and playing musical instruments children are involved in working and cooperating with their peers and adults. Singing with a class of peers is a good way of establishing confidence to use one's voice in front of a group and to hear the sound of one's own voice, thus building confidence in oral communication. Toddlers can feel a wonderful freedom to express themselves walking in the outdoors or being carried on an adult's shoulders singing well-known songs, chants and rhymes as loudly as they wish. Music enhances group work skills, working together to produce a sound through song or chant. Playing musical instruments with peers also requires working together as a group so that communication and interaction skills, essential to literacy development, are developed through musical activities. Music may also contribute to emotional development as children become aware of 'happy' and 'sad' music in major and minor keys. They also learn about using words with music to express different emotions, so enhancing their emotional and self-awareness.

So, it is now recognised that even in their first year, young children can use musical skills to engage with the world socially and for cognitive development (Adachi and Trehub, 2012, in Young, 2016). It is also widely recognised that the child is not just a passive recipient in this development process but actively participates in it (Young and Ilari, 2012, in Young, 2016).

REFLECTION: LEARNING THROUGH MUSIC

■ Identify and reflect on a children's song or rhyme. Consider how it could be used to enhance different aspects of learning

■ Consider a musical activity that could contribute to communicating and working with peers

---

Having considered some of the ways in which specific aspects of sensory experience and learning contribute to learning and development, it is important to think about how such experiences can be inclusive, particularly for children with special educational needs and/or disabilities (SEND). The following section explores some of the benefits and challenges associated with sensory learning for such children.

Implications for practice: sensory learning and inclusion

Clearly the benefits of sensory learning outlined above may not be experienced by all children in the same way. Each child is different and for some children in the early years particular sensory experiences may be very stressful and unhelpful. For others, sensory experiences may not lead to learning in ways that we might expect. The social model of disability and philosophies of inclusion have ensured that Special Educational Needs and Disability (SEND) policy in England focuses on meeting children's needs in inclusive mainstream environments wherever possible (Cunnah, 2012). One of the key issues stated in the SEND Code of Practice is that the UK government is 'committed to inclusive education of disabled children' and 'the progressive removal of barriers to learning and participation in mainstream education' (DfE and DoH, 2015:25). The responsibility for achieving successful inclusion lies with early years leaders.

> The leaders of early years settings ... should establish and maintain a culture of high expectations that expects those working with children ... with SEN or disabilities to include them in all the opportunities available to other children and young people so they can achieve well.
>
> (DfE and DoH, 2015:27)

However, inclusion is a difficult term to define and consequently even more difficult to implement (Cunnah, 2012). Nutbrown and Clough (2006) interpreted it as the 'drive towards maximal participation and minimal exclusion from early years settings'. They noted the fact that,

> given that in practice 'inclusion' can only have an operational rather than conceptual meaning, it is clear that there are as many 'versions' of inclusion as there are early years settings – or, indeed, the individuals who make up those particular cultures of living and learning.
>
> (Nutbrown and Clough, 2006:3)

One of the challenges in including all children in early years settings in sensory learning is that for some children over-exposure to sensory experiences, for example loud music or music combined with clapping and singing, may be extremely stressful. For others, over-sensitivity to light and colour may result in classroom environments being overly stimulating. Similarly, ordinary everyday smells and odours may be quite pungent and repulsive for some children. The term 'Sensory Processing Disorder' has recently emerged, referring to children who may over or under react to sensory stimuli. As such, early years classrooms and environments that are replete with sensory experiences and learning opportunities for most children may be very exclusionary environments for other children. They may even provoke aggressive behaviours or avoidance tactics. Peer and Reid (2012:105) note four common difficulties with sensory experiences including:

- Hyper (over) sensitivity, for example distress at loud noises and discomfort or irritation with certain textures

- Hypo (under) sensitivity, for example not responding to pain, heat or their name being called and reduced discrimination of tactile information

- Somatodyspraxia – poor tactile and proprioceptive processing which can result in clumsiness, falling, bumping into objects, poor fine motor skills and poor organisation

- Gravitational insecurity that is caused by a fear of movement, for example unwillingness to engage in gross motor play

The Code of Practice for SEND identifies four categories of impairment, one of which is sensory/physical impairment.

> Many children and young people with vision impairment (VI), hearing impairment (HI) or a multi-sensory impairment (MSI) will require specialist support and/or equipment to access their learning, or habilitation support. Children and young people with an MSI have a combination of vision and hearing difficulties.
>
> (DfE and DoH, 2015:98)

Thus, while some children respond differently to sensory stimuli, some may have sensory impairments, for example visual or hearing impairments. Children with multi-sensory impairment, for example congenitally deafblind children, may experience sensory deprivation and subsequently opportunities for understanding and learning are potentially more limited (van Dijk and Nelson, 1998, in Miller and Hodges, 2005). Similarly, children with physical impairments may not be able to feel and experience sensory stimulation in the same way as children who do not have such impairments.

For other children who have not been diagnosed with a sensory impairment, significant difficulties emerge when processing sensory information. Sensory processing involves registering, organising and interpreting information from sight, smell, touch, taste, hearing, somatic senses, vestibular and proprioceptors. Some children who do not necessarily have vision or hearing impairments have problems with auditory discrimination so that deciphering sounds and rhymes is problematic. For others, visual discrimination is challenging so that seeing the differences between letters and words is not always clear. Therefore, using sensory experiences to promote learning is not without issues for some children in the early years and may sometimes be more exclusionary than inclusive.

As noted earlier, effective processing of sensory information contributes to cognitive, physical, emotional and social development. It is clear, therefore, that children who struggle with processing sensory experiences will not develop in the same ways as their peers who can process this information. This may result in issues around behaviour as:

> Efficient and effective sensory processing has an essential role to play in the ability to regulate arousal and attention levels, and in controlling

emotional and behavioural control. If sensory information is perceived inaccurately, faulty sensory integration occurs.

(Peer and Reid, 2012:105)

Clearly the impact of impaired sensory processing is evident on developing independence, for example eating and dressing. This can result in frustration and embarrassment and ultimately social isolation. Lack of fine motor skills affects writing and writing speed. Poor gross motor skill development leads to problems engaging in games and not 'fitting in' with peer activities.

It is acknowledged that inclusion of all children in the early years in sensory learning is challenging, and that philosophies around inclusive education often meet with tensions at the point of implementation (Brown and Palaiologou, 2016). However, the SEND Code of Practice (DfE and DoH, 2015) makes it clear that early years practitioners are responsible for meeting the needs of all children:

All early years providers have duties under the Equality Act 2010. In particular, they must not discriminate against, harass or victimise disabled children, and they must make reasonable adjustments, including the provision of auxiliary aids and services for disabled children, to prevent them being put at substantial disadvantage. This duty is anticipatory – it requires thought to be given in advance to what disabled children and young people might require and what adjustments might need to be made to prevent that disadvantage.

(DfE and DoH, 2015:80–81)

Some researchers have proposed overcoming some of these issues through multi-sensory approaches to learning. Reid stated 'It is now well established that learning is more effective for learners with dyslexia if it is multisensory' (2013:11). Multi-sensory learning involves a learning environment that accommodates visual, auditory and kinaesthetic and tactile learning preferences. The aim is to use every sensory pathway to the brain so that no opportunity for sensory stimulation is missed. Thus, for children in whom one or more sensory pathways is impaired, other sensory routes are employed. For example, a child who is finding it difficult to discriminate sounds and letters in words may find it helpful to use kinaesthetic sensory stimulation. As such, feeling letter shapes, writing letters in sand, feeling a letter written by someone else's finger on their back or writing letters in the air may provide a sensory stimulus and aid their development in sound and letter discrimination. Multi-sensory approaches have been used in order to include as many children as possible in mainstream classrooms. Some have recommended using a 'sensory diet'. A 'sensory diet' is an individually focused programme which addresses sensory needs, helping children to pay attention, learn more effectively and be less distracted but this has no evidence base: 'With incomplete and contradictory findings from research, the field lacks consensus as to what sensory interventions families should seek and practitioners can recommend' (Case-Smith, Weaver and Fristad, 2015:135).

However, some researchers argue that learning is so individualised for some learners that a mainstream environment is not necessarily appropriate for all learners (Farrell, 2014). Others have warned about focusing on learning styles (Claxton, 2008).

VIGNETTE: AN INDIVIDUAL APPROACH

Lawrence is five years old and is not making the progress his teacher would normally expect for his age. He has no known visual, hearing or physical impairment. When he enters the classroom setting he seems to become agitated by the noise and activity of children entering and settling down and finds it difficult to settle down himself. During an activity when children are required to work with playdough he is reluctant to participate and will not touch the playdough. During a music session he runs out of the classroom, putting his hands over his ears when he hears the sound of a drum. During the outdoor play sessions Lawrence is very reticent to join in activities, particularly the climbing frame.

■ What aspects of Lawrence's behaviour would be of concern to his teacher?

■ Why do you think Lawrence is responding in these ways to certain sensory stimuli?

■ What sort of sensory diet may be useful to support Lawrence in his learning?

This section has highlighted some of the tensions and issues associated with sensory experiences and learning in early years classrooms and the challenge of inclusion for some children. However, there are other tensions related to including sensory experiences in the early years which will now be examined.

Tensions and issues associated with sensory learning

Some of the tensions and issues associated with including all children in sensory learning have been articulated above. It is clear from current guidance that early years practitioners have a responsibility to ensure inclusive provision in their settings. Consequently, adults' knowledge and understanding of children's sensory experiences and learning, ability to apply strategies to enhance such learning and flexible approach are key to healthy child development. Another aspect to consider is how far adults should allow free play and child-led exploration, or whether a more structured, adult-supported approach is necessary to gain the most potential development from sensory experiences. Not all practitioners are equally confident in supporting sensory learning. Some adults find it challenging to link pedagogy to sensory learning and professional training programmes are not necessarily preparing people for this aspect of their work. All this is compounded by a goal orientated curriculum in England and a focus on standards which limits practitioner flexibility in activity selection (Santer et al., 2007).

> What passed as education by 2016, and was fuelled by dropping down in international league tables, was an elaborate system of tests and examinations in a government-decreed subject centred curriculum. From phonics tests and early years assessments for children as young as four, to the endless presentation of information as to who was failing ...
>
> (Tomlinson, 2017:92)

It is also evident that, while musical experiences contribute significantly to child development, not all children experience or engage in musical activities in the same way. Musical experiences are subject to diverse social, cultural and environmental contexts. Hence children's musical experiences take place with different access to resources and activities. They are also influenced by the diverse values, expectations and aspirations of the adults around them. For example, children living in socially deprived areas may have less access to music sessions and experiences than those whose parents pay for extra-curricular tuition for them. Similarly, children from diverse cultural backgrounds appreciate musical experiences differently. Finally, putting research into practice is challenging when early years practitioners are under pressure from the demands of their institutions and roles, and are not always confident to incorporate musical activities into the curriculum (Young, 2016).

While the many benefits for learning and development associated with learning outdoors have been stated above, some have raised questions about definitional confusion around the term 'outdoor learning' and what it really means. Just because children are experiencing the outdoors does not necessarily mean that pedagogical approaches in the outdoor environment are giving more choice and enjoyment for learners. Research (Waite, 2011:79) has identified the pressures of 'external requirements' and 'conflict between personal aspirations and practice, the ideal and the real'. Similarly, Maynard and Waters (2007) were concerned that practitioners may employ the same teaching and learning strategies outdoors as they do indoors, focusing on subject knowledge and skills. Just because children are 'outside' does not necessarily mean that they are in a 'natural environment'. Also, many early years settings are located in inner city environments with limited access to natural environments and not all natural environments are safe places for children to explore. In an era of high risk awareness and litigation in England many practitioners and settings may prefer to keep children safe rather than allow free exploration in natural outdoor environments.

> **REFLECTION:** BARRIERS TO SENSORY LEARNING
>
> ■ Consider barriers to sensory learning that you have experienced or are aware of
>
> ■ Provide examples of how such barriers could be overcome

Conclusion

Thus, it is clear that sensory experiences and sensory learning contribute positively to many aspects of child development in the early years. However, there are many tensions and issues that impede these positive effects for some children. These issues and tensions may arise from the child's own preferences, disposition and impairments, for example multi-sensory impairments. However, issues are more likely to arise from practitioners and settings which lack the resources, knowledge, skills or confidence to support such experiences and learning effectively. Added to this, a focus on standards and goals in early years often leads to different priorities among practitioners, and fears of litigation result in a strongly risk-averse educational environment.

Adults working with very young children need to be trained and prepared to understand the value of sensory learning and engage flexibly with a range of diverse approaches and strategies. It is also incumbent on leaders of early years settings to understand and engage with the diverse socio-cultural responses to sensory learning opportunities in an increasingly multicultural early years population. Finally, studies in neuroscience are constantly advancing our knowledge and understanding of the impact of sensory learning on brain development. We need to ensure that such research reaches early years practitioners so that a research-informed profession is in place for the future.

References

Adachi, M. & Trehub, S.E. (2012) Musical lives of infants. In G. McPherson & G. Welch (eds), *The Oxford Handbook of Music Education*. New York, NY: Oxford University Press.

Adams, M., Foorman, B., Lundberg, I. & Beeler, T. (2002) *Phonemic Awareness in Young Children*. Baltimore, MD: Paul H. Brookes Publishing Co.

Anvari, S., Trainor, L., Woodside, J. & Levy, B. (2002) Relations among musical skills, phonological processing and early reading ability in preschool children. *Journal of Experimental Child Psychology*, 83 (2), 111–130.

Astley, N., Baker, M. and Hall, P. (2004) *Peppa Pig*. Channel 5.

Bilton, H. (2002) *Outdoor Play in the Early Years*. London: David Fulton.

Blakeslee, M. & Blakeslee, S. (2007) *The Body Has a Mind of Its Own.* New York: Random House.

Blythe, S.G. (2004) *The Well Balanced Child: Movement and Early Learning.* Stroud: Hawthorn Press.

Brierley, J. (1994) *Give Me a Child Until He is Seven.* Sussex: Falmer Press.

Brown, T. & Jernigan, T. (2012) Brain development in the preschool years. *Neuropsychology Review,* 22 (4), 313–333.

Brown, Z. & Palaiologou, I. (2016) Inclusive practice in early childhood education. In Z. Brown (ed.), *Inclusive Education: Perspectives on Pedagogy, Policy and Practice.* Oxon: Routledge.

Bruner, J. (1960) *The Process of Education.* Harvard: Harvard University Press.

Buchanan, L. (2012) Animal hand-clap rap. Online at: http://www.songsforteaching.com/store/animal-hand-clap-rap-without-childrens-voices--pr-58794.html

Burack, J. (2005) Uniting mind and music: Shaw's vision continues. *American Music Teacher,* 55 (1), 84–87.

Case-Smith, J., Weaver, L. & Fristad, M. (2015) A systematic review of sensory processing interventions for children with autism spectrum disorders. *Autism,* 19 (2), 133–148.

Chau, C. & Riforgiate, T. (2010) *Child Development Senior Project Spring Quarter.* San Louis Obispo: California State University.

Chugani, H.T. (1998) A critical period of brain development: Studies of cerebral glucose utilization with PET. *Preventive Medicine,* 27, 184–188.

Claxton, G. (2008) *What's the Point of School?* Oxford: Oneworld.

Cunnah, W. (2012) *What Social Model? Disabled Students' Experience of Work-Related Learning and Placements.* PhD Thesis: Sheffield Hallam University.

DfE & DoH (2015) *Special Educational Needs and Disability Code of Practice: 0 to 25 Years.* London: HMSO. Online at: https://www.gov.uk/government/publications/send-code-of-practice-0-to-25

Farrell, M. (2014) *Looking into Special Education: A Synthesis of Key Themes and Concepts.* Oxon: Routledge.

Fjortoft, I. (2001) The natural environment as a playground for children: The impact of outdoor play activities in pre-primary school children. *Early Childhood Education Journal,* 29 (2), 111–117.

Fjortoft, I. (2004) Landscape as playscape: The effects of natural environments on children's play and motor development. *Children, Youth and Environments,* 14 (2), 21–44.

Gardner, H. (1983) *Frames of Mind.* New York: Basic Books.

Geist, K., Geist, E.A. & Kuznik, K. (2012) The patterns of music: Young children learning mathematics through beat, rhythm and melody. *Young Children,* January 2012, 74–79.

Goldschmied, E. & Jackson, S. (1994) *People Under Three: Young Children in Day Care.* London: Routledge.

Griffiths, J. (2003) Do little children need big brains? *Early Education,* Summer, 7–8.

Gromko, J. (2005) The effect of music instruction on phonemic awareness in beginning readers. *Journal of Research in Music Education,* 53 (3), 199–209.

Hyde, K., Lerch, J., Norton, A., Forgeard, M., Winner, E., Evans, A. & Schlaug, G. (2009) Musical training shapes structural brain development. *Journal of Neuroscience,* 29 (10), 3019–3025.

Janks, H. (2010) *Literacy and Power.* New York: Routledge.

Lebedeva, G. (2015) Building brains one relationship at a time. *Exchange,* 11, Nov/Dec 2015, 21–25.

Linder, S., Powers-Costello, B. & Stegelin, B. (2011) Mathematics in early childhood: Research-based rational and practical strategies. *Early Childhood Education Journal*, 39 (1), 29–37.

Lindon, J. (2005) *Understanding Child Development: Linking Theory and Practice.* Oxon: Hodder Education.

Louv, R. (2010) *Last Child in the Woods: Saving Our Children From Nature-Deficit Disorder.* London: Atlantic Books.

Maynard, T. & Waters, J. (2007) Learning in the outdoor environment: A missed opportunity? *Early Years*, 27 (3) October 2007, 255–265.

McKendrick, J.H. (2005) *School grounds in Scotland: Research Report*, Scottish Poverty Information Unit. Online at: http://www.sportscotland.org.uk

Miller, O. & Hodges, L. (2005) Deafblindness. In A. Lewis and B. Norwich (eds), *Special Teaching for Special Children? Pedagogies for Inclusion.* Maidenhead: OU Press.

Moreno, S., Marques, C., Santos, A., Santos, M., Castro, S. & Besson, M. (2009) Musical training influences linguistic abilities in 8-year-old children: More evidence for brain plasticity. *Cerebral Cortex, 19* (3), 712–723.

Nutbrown, C. & Clough, P. (2006) *Inclusion in the Early Years.* London: Sage.

Ouvry, M. (2003) *Exercising Muscles and Minds: Outdoor Play and the Early Years Curriculum.* London: Jessica Kingsley.

Peer, L. & Reid, G. (2012) *Special Educational Needs: A Guide for Inclusive Practice.* London: Sage.

Piaget, J. (1971) *Biology and Knowledge.* Chicago: University of Chicago Press.

Pound, L. (2008) *How Children Learn: From Montessori to Vygotsky.* London: Practical Pre-School Books.

Pound, L. (2009) *How Children Learn 3: Contemporary Thinking and Theorists.* London: Practical Pre-School Books.

Reid, G. (2013) *Dyslexia and Inclusion*, 2nd edition. London: David Fulton.

Santer, J., Griffiths, C. with Goodall, D. (2007) *Making Space for Free Play in Early Childhood: A Literature Review.* London: Play England.

Schiller, P. (2008) Songs and rhymes as a springboard to literacy. *Early Childhood News.* Online at: http://www.earlychildhoodnews.com/earlychildhood/article_home. aspx?ArticleID=478

Siraj-Blatchford, J. & Siraj-Blatchford, I. (2002) Discriminating between schemes and schemas in young children's emergent learning of science and technology. *International Journal of Early Years Education*, 10 (3), 205–214.

Standards and Testing Agency (2016) *Early Years Foundation Stage Profile: 2017 Handbook.* Online at: https://www.gov.uk/government/uploads/system/uploads/ attachment_data/file/564249/2017_EYFSP_handbook_v1.1.pdf

Stephenson, A. (2003) Physical risk-taking: Dangerous or endangered? *Early Years*, 23(1), 35–43.

Street, C. (2002) Play and education. *Highlight*, 195. National Children's Bureau.

Tarbert, K. (2012) Learning literacy through music. *Oneota Reading Journal.* Luther College. Online at: http://www.luther.edu/oneota-reading-journal/archive/2012/ learning-literacy-through-music/

Tomlinson, S. (2017) *A Sociology of Special and Inclusive Education: Exploring the Manufacture of Inability.* Oxon: Routledge.

Tovey, H. (2007) *Playing Outdoors: Spaces and Places, Risk and Challenge.* Maidenhead: OU Press.

van Dijk, J. & Nelson, C. (1998) History and change in the education of children who are deaf-blind since the rubella outbreak of the 1960s: The influence of methods developed in the Netherlands. *Deaf-blind Perspectives*, 5 (2), 1–5.

Waite, S. (ed.) (2011) *Children Learning Outside the Classroom: From Birth to Eleven.* London: Sage.

Waite, S., Davies, B. & Brown, K. (2006) *Five Stories of Outdoor Learning from Settings for 2–11 Year Olds in Devon.* Plymouth: University of Plymouth.

Young, S. (2016) Early childhood music education research: An overview. *Research Studies in Music Education*, 38 (1), 9–21.

Young, S. & Ilari, B. (2012) Musical participation from birth to three: Toward a global perspective. In G. McPherson & G. Welch (eds), *Oxford Handbook of Music Education.* New York, NY: Oxford University Press.

5 Social learning

OVERVIEW OF THE CHAPTER

This chapter is about social learning in early childhood contexts, focusing on:

- Understandings and theories associated with social learning

- Why social learning is important and how this is reflected in current documentation

- The value of social learning in child development

- The issues and tensions related to social learning with specific reference to socio-cultural diversity, gender and children for whom social learning is challenging

Introduction

This chapter focuses on social learning in the early years. Previous chapters have explored emotional and sensory learning, but all learning takes place in social contexts, including relationships with people and the environment. This chapter examines a range of issues related to social learning in the early years. What is social learning and why is it important? How can social learning contribute to child development? How does social learning affect identity formation, gender, morals, values, attitudes and beliefs? What sorts of challenges emerge for early years practitioners when implementing social learning, particularly in diverse socio-cultural contexts and with children who experience challenges in this area?

What is social learning?

Young children develop socially at an amazing pace during the first six years of their life. However, this development takes place at varying paces for different children (Dowling, 2014). The development of social competence in children in the early years is crucial. 'Relationships are at the centre of learning' (Lebedeva, 2015:22) and 'Social knowledge is the foundation of children's learning in pre-school' (Williams, Sheridan and Sandberg, 2014:236). Ashdown and Bernard (2012) highlighted research that demonstrates the ways in which social-emotional competence, along with cognition, are very important predictors of academic achievement. Children grow up within particular social contexts and settings in which they interact with and form relationships with a range of children, peers and adults. These begin within their home environment where they interact with parents, carers, siblings and others in their wider family and community. Later, in early years settings, children begin to interact with and develop relationships with professional adults and peers.

Children's learning is complex. We have already discussed some aspects of emotional and sensory learning in Chapters 3 and 4 and social learning does not take place in isolation from other aspects of learning. Bennett (2004, cited in Williams et al., 2014) identified two approaches to preschool. The first of these, the 'social pedagogic approach', concentrates on enabling children to become active citizens with a strong sense of identity and self-esteem which enables them to have control over their own lives. The second approach is referred to as the 'pre-primary approach' which is more focused on cognitive development in preparation for school. Clearly both approaches are equally important and indeed complimentary, so need to be seen as part of a holistic approach to learning. 'Children learn by experiencing, acting in and communicating with the environment, which in turn interacts with them in various ways' (Williams et al., 2014). It is not possible to separate children's cognitive, social and emotional learning and development because they are inseparably linked. Learning in the early years 'is understood as a process where children, peers, teachers and families are actively, authentically and meaningfully engaged in relational co-construction of knowledge and skills' (Langford, 2010:121, in Jonsdottir and Coleman, 2014). In other words, learning is social and takes place within relationships. It is useful to consider the ways in which key theorists have understood social learning.

Theories related to social learning

In the 1960s Albert Bandura put forward a theory of social learning. For Bandura, the observations that children make of adults and other children were significant predictors of their own behaviour, because children model behaviours that they observe. Watching adult behaviour enables children to see what is acceptable and desired behaviour. Bandura viewed children as learning and imitating not only behaviours but also ideas, expectations and standards. He believed that reinforcement strengthens behaviours. As such, social learning theory builds on behaviourist theories to demonstrate that feelings, observation and thinking about experiences contribute to learning (Lindon, 2005).

Lev Vygotsky is the founder of the social constructivist approach to learning. He viewed the social context of learning as vital and saw language as a social tool. He regarded learning as 'a process within social interactions' (Lindon, 2005:40). Vygotsky advocated the Zone of Proximal Development (ZPD), an area of potential learning that children may achieve through social interaction with adults and other children. For Vygotsky language is social in origin, arising from a child's interactions with adults and other children. As such, language emanates from and leads to social interaction. As children observe they do not just respond to words but interpret aspects of the context and facial expression and body language in order to comprehend situations (Pound, 2008). For example, a young child may recognise that an adult is unhappy with their table manners by their reprimands but, additionally, through observing their unhappy facial expressions. Thus, Vygotsky viewed interactions with adults, families, communities and other children as essential in child development. He saw the working together of social and cognitive development as crucial.

Bruner (1960) also viewed language as an important tool for adults to employ in order to extend children's thinking and understanding. While he favoured a child-centred approach to learning, and thought that children learn mainly through play, he stated that adult participation or 'scaffolding' enhanced understanding (Lindon, 2005).

Bronfenbrenner (1979, 1986) studied the impact of the environment on children's learning and produced an 'ecological systems theory'. He took a socio-cultural approach and stated that children are indirectly affected by the social and cultural system in which they grow up. For example, culture, faith, economic policy and adult employment patterns all have an impact on children's lives in different ways. Bronfenbrenner stated that children do not grow up in isolation, they interact with the environment in a complex set of layers that include a 'microsystem', an 'exosystem' and a 'macrosystem'.

Everyday interactions with family, friends and peers at home, and in early years settings, all occur within the microsystem. However, it is not just these close and familiar relationships and environments that have an impact on children's social learning. The larger exosystem of the neighbourhood and community social networks also affect social learning in the early years. For example, parents' friends and contacts, their employment or lack of it and the pressures the family may face from being employed or unemployed. Children may also be involved in local groups in the community which they attend less frequently than their early years setting but which contribute to their social learning and development. Finally, Bronfenbrenner identified the macrosystem to include wider social structures like the education system, the economic situation and system, and cultural values which indirectly affect social competence. For example, the current state of the economy affects the relative wealth or poverty in the family. A child brought up in the relatively strong London economy may not have the same social experiences as a child brought up in poorer areas of the UK where unemployment and poverty are more evident. Similarly, the predominant ethnicity, culture, faith and values of the society in which children grow up feed into their sense of identity (Lindon, 2005; Pound, 2009).

Social competences are also time bound. Children whose early years experiences took place in the 1950s, for example, when there was no such thing as internet, social media and mobile phones, had quite different socio-cultural experiences from those whose early years experiences took place in the twenty-first century. Similarly, socio-cultural experiences are shaped by geography, or the place in which they happen. A child whose early years experiences took place in Eastern Europe, for example, would not experience the same socio-cultural context as a child whose early years experiences occurred in the UK. In the current situation where the movement of people is far more evident than it was fifty years ago, socio-cultural experiences become more complex as children have often experienced a range of early years contexts in their lives.

In diverse socio-cultural situations children are faced with different expectations from the adults in their families and educational settings. Their social experiences are unique to them. They are also offered different opportunities to practice what is valued most in specific socio-cultural settings. For example, girls from Gypsy Roma Traveller cultures are often encouraged to learn and practise a domestic role. Thus, education is not necessarily the main priority for girls in some communities. Similarly, children from families with a strong religious faith may be encouraged to learn and practise aspects of their parents' faith. These religious values and practices may well take priority over other national educational goals.

So, it is evident that all these socio-cultural experiences are set within the context of socio-cultural goals and values. In the UK these goals are expressed within the Statutory Framework for EYFS (DfE, 2017) and the EYFS Profile (STA, 2016). The following section explores the importance of social learning as expressed in these documents and some of the implications for positive identity formation and self-esteem in young children.

Why is social learning important?

The Statutory Framework for the Early Years Foundation Stage (EYFS) (DfE, 2017:6) emphasises the crucial influence of social interactions with people and the environment. It contains four guiding principles, one of which is that 'children learn to be strong and independent through positive relationships'. Another guiding principle states that 'children learn and develop well in enabling environments, in which their experiences respond to their individual needs and there is a strong partnership between practitioners and parents and/ or carers' (DfE, 2017:6). The framework reflects Vygotsky's view that learning takes place within the context of social interaction. It also reflects his and Bruner's view that children's potential learning is harnessed and extended through adult interaction and support. Children learn with the people who care for them and have their best interests at heart.

The Statutory Framework outlines seven areas of learning that are identified as crucial in shaping educational programmes in early years settings. It recognises the interconnectedness of learning as a holistic whole, but puts particular emphasis on the view that 'Three areas are particularly crucial for igniting children's curiosity and enthusiasm for learning, and for building their capacity to learn, form relationships and thrive' (DfE, 2017:7). The three main areas stipulated are communication and language, physical development, and personal, social and emotional development. As such the emphasis on social learning through communication and social-emotional development reflects the value placed on social learning in the early years in England. It emphasises the need to give children the opportunity to be involved in rich language environments, speaking and listening in various situations, so gaining confidence and skills in expressing themselves.

> Personal, social and emotional development involves helping children to develop a positive sense of themselves, and others; to form positive relationships and develop respect for others; to develop social skills and learn how to manage their feelings; to understand appropriate behaviour in groups; and to have confidence in their own abilities.
>
> (DfE, 2017:8)

The emphasis on the importance of adult interactions is further enhanced by the requirement for early years settings to assign a key person for children in their care. The role of the key person is to liaise with parents and support them in the child's development at home. They are expected to ensure a focus on the child as an individual and help families engage with specialist support where necessary. Elfer, Goldschmied and Selleck (2012) consider the key worker as different from the 'key person' so draw a distinction between the roles. While the key worker is important in performing the role of liaison, organisation and coordination between home and setting, the 'key person' is more about someone who is daily involved with the child and thus of emotional significance to the child. The key person is there to make children feel that they are valued and loved by someone when they are away from their home surroundings so that they will feel part of a close and affectionate relationship. Dowling (2014) commented that the family has a profound effect on a child's sense of identity. However, when they move to an early years setting the professionals in that setting share the responsibility for establishing positive identities in young children. She argued that the key person is one of the 'significant others' with an emotional link and a profound effect on the positive self-esteem of young children (Dowling, 2014:12).

> The Key Persons approach is a way of working in early years settings in which the whole focus and organization is aimed at enabling and supporting close attachments between individual children and individual practitioners. The Key Persons approach is an involvement, an individual and reciprocal commitment between a member of staff and a family. It is an approach that has clear benefits for all involved.
>
> (Elfer et al., 2012:23)

Social learning and self-esteem

Hence, the importance of social learning in the early years is emphasised in the Statutory Framework for EYFS. The DfE (2017:8) emphasis on personal, social and emotional development highlights 'helping children to develop a positive sense of themselves, and others; to form positive relationships and develop respect for others'. Once a child has established their own identity they are in a place to develop self-esteem which is about putting a value on that identity (Dowling, 2014). If children are to learn social skills and competences, they need to develop self-esteem so that they are able to listen to and respect the views and opinions of others. Self-esteem empowers children to speak up for themselves and express their own perspectives (Williams et al., 2014).

Social learning, then, is vital for children to develop positive self-identities. Identity includes the way in which children see themselves, how they see themselves in relation to others and how others view them. How children perceive themselves and how they think others perceive them is very powerful, and has an impact on their self-esteem (Cunnah, 2012, 2015).

> Identity is our understanding of who we are and of who other people are, and, reciprocally, other people's understandings of themselves and of others (which includes us).
>
> (Jenkins, 2004:5)

Clearly, children's sense of identity emanates from their relationships with people, and their environments. Positive social relationships with adults at home, in educational settings and in their communities, contribute to children's positive self-identities and so positive sense of themselves. For example, adults who encourage children with frequent, specific praise help them to develop a positive sense of themselves. Adults who model positive social interactions and positive attitudes to other adults and children encourage children to respect others and form positive relationships with them.

In relation to Bronfenbrenner's ecological systems theory, the wider society, including socio-cultural factors, contributes to children's positive views of themselves and of others. If the community or society in which a child grows up holds positive attitudes to difference and diversity, children are more likely to develop social competences around celebrating diversity. If they are surrounded by discriminatory attitudes and prejudice they are more likely to become prejudiced themselves.

> Identity is at the interface between the personal, that is the thoughts, feelings, personal histories, and the social, that is the societies in which we live and the social, cultural and economic factors which shape experience and make it possible for people to take up some identities and render others inaccessible or impossible.
>
> (Woodward, 2000, in Swain and French, 2008:67)

Fortunately, negative and destructive identities are not fixed because identities change in diverse situations and timeframes. Identity is a social construction so can be challenged and transformed (Jenkins, 2004). 'Self-esteem is not fixed; it can change according to the people we are with and the situations we find ourselves in' (Dowling, 2014:12). Hence, even children who have experienced negative social experiences that may have had a negative impact on their sense of themselves and others can overcome adversity with the help of others. In Chapter 1 we explored different sets of principles about early childhood. The Center on the Developing Child at Harvard University, for example, includes the principle that young children who have been exposed to adversity do not invariably develop stress-related disorders. There is no place for predeterminist perspectives since the brain continues to develop well into adolescence and early adulthood. Baker et al. (2014) found that strong relationships between children and their teachers, for example, could change a child's life chances, and could help children to gain higher aspirations.

REFLECTION: PLAY AND SOCIAL LEARNING

- Identify experiences or aspects of play in the early years that enhance the social aspect of learning

- Reflect on examples of promoting positive identities in young children

- How do the experiences and examples above relate to the Statutory Framework for EYFS?

Children, therefore, construct their own identity. They begin with their personal perspective and work outwards towards the wider social networks of family and community. It is essential that they build this sense of themselves and their own self-worth before they can understand the sources of identity of others (Lindon, 2005).

The impact of social learning on morals, values and attitudes

> Young children should be helped to understand about right and wrong and to eventually develop their own moral code, rather than simply be encouraged to comply with adult requirements to behave properly ... Children's behaviour is influenced by their temperament, through their observations of others and through their feelings and physical needs.
>
> (Dowling, 2014:148)

Educationists hold diverse views about appropriate behaviour and how such behaviours are acquired. The Early Years Foundation Stage Profile (STA, 2016) states that children should be able to manage their feelings and behaviour. Children should have opportunities to talk about their own behaviour and the behaviour of others and its consequences. They should understand rules and boundaries and why some behaviours are unacceptable. Bandura related children's behaviours to the adults that they observe and imitate. He also viewed children's motivation to make things happen as enabling them to take control of their behaviours. Vygotsky believed that children imitate the behaviours of their social contacts in life, constructing rules as they play, assuming different roles. For Bronfenbrenner, a range of environmental issues can affect a child's approach to behaviour. In the 'microsystem' positive models of behaviour at home and early years settings will have a positive impact on the child's behaviour, while negative models of selfish and aggressive behaviours will have the opposite effect. The 'exosystem' may have negative effects on the child's behaviour, for example if a parent leaves home. Within the 'macrosystem' the loss of valued services may lead to negative behaviours (Dowling, 2014).

Positive early relationships motivate children to please and to get on well with others, so developing a sense of what is right and wrong. So, for example, a child will not wish to displease a parent or upset a friend through inappropriate behaviours. While the child may not fully comprehend the description of what they are doing wrong, for example 'bullying' or 'grabbing', they are likely to understand the negative body language and facial expressions disapproving of their behaviours.

Getting attuned to the feelings of others is referred to as pro-social behaviour or empathy. This may include altruism where children become concerned for the welfare of others (Lindon, 2005). For example, a young child may share her snack with a sibling who is upset at not having one or a child may give his teddy bear to a child who is crying. As such, children learn acceptable boundaries and rules through the necessity of working in relationships with adults and children and also through modelling the behaviours of others.

Clearly different adults have varied expectations around children's behaviours and so set different examples and models. For example, some parents model and encourage behaviours that are exemplified in their religious faith while others may wish their children to cope through a defensive and aggressive approach to behaviour. Different cultures often have different approaches to encouraging and developing appropriate behaviours so that in some cultures it is still acceptable and encouraged to use corporal punishment to deter inappropriate behaviours. Dowling (2014:152–153) referred to 'permissive', 'negotiated' and 'directed' approaches to managing behaviours. The 'permissive' approach allows children free rein to decide what is appropriate behaviour for themselves. In the 'negotiated' approach adults provide authoritative boundaries but explain the reasons for these rules and in loving relationships children develop a desire to please. The 'directed' approach is much more authoritarian, relying on punishments and rewards or emotional blackmail.

As children experience varied role models and approaches to behaviour they learn what are acceptable behaviours, morals, values and attitudes. Collaboration provides many opportunities for learning to engage appropriately with others.

Collaboration and social learning

Most learning in the early years takes place in contexts where children are interacting and collaborating with adults and peers. Collaborating with others involves listening, talking, solving problems and responding emotionally to oneself and others. Children begin to learn emotional responses with their parents at home, where they begin to model the ways in which parents handle feelings. They also learn from other significant adults in their lives like grandparents, carers and early years professionals. In order to engage effectively in these relationships, it is essential for children to learn to collaborate with others. In collaborating with other adults and children, young children learn about teamwork, justice and fair play. They have to communicate, share, think, care about those they are collaborating with, adapt to the different demands of the group and collaborate to solve problems in order to achieve goals. All these skills are developed while collaborating with others in social contexts. As such, collaboration has the potential to enhance social learning in many ways.

The preschool context is a very useful setting for young children to learn to interact, communicate and collaborate. During the course of such collaboration it is essential to listen to and learn how to respect the opinions of others. In such situations, conflicts may need to be resolved and democratic principles employed. Young children will also need to develop self-esteem and the confidence to voice their own views and opinions, and collaborating with others offers opportunities for children to develop social skills in all these areas (Williams et al., 2014).

In collaboration with and relating to others children acquire emotional intelligence as they learn to understand and control their feelings and understand the feelings and emotions of others. An emotionally intelligent child demonstrates skills of self-awareness, empathy, impulse control, listening, decision-making and anger management (Pound, 2008). In his theory of multiple intelligences Howard Gardner (1993) stated that individuals have two personal intelligences. These include, firstly, intrapersonal intelligence, which enables individuals to reflect on themselves. Secondly, interpersonal intelligence enables individuals to interact effectively with others. A significant benefit of collaboration is the learning and development of such awareness of and appropriate response to the needs of others.

Hence it is clear that children develop a range of understanding and skills through collaboration with adults and other children. However, social learning is complicated because understandings of what are appropriate social skills and competences vary in diverse cultural contexts. Also, some children find communication, collaboration and social learning challenging.

Tensions and issues associated with social learning: social justice

> Children's behaviour and their development are not changed directly by social class and poverty. Children are affected by the attitudes, experiences, and stresses that reach them through parents and the important adults in their lives.
>
> (Lindon, 2005:248)

Social justice concerns all forms of diversity including gender, ethnicity, culture, faith, class, social backgrounds and children identified with SEND (special educational needs and/or disabilities). The Equality Act 2010 (2015) cites 'protected characteristics', including race, ethnicity, religion, sex and sexual orientation. Children exhibit differences from their peers because of cultural, religious or traditional expectations so that 'identity is concerned not only with behaviour but with physical appearance' (Goepel, Childerhouse and Sharpe, 2014:26). Children who dress differently because of religious traditions, or who look different because of a physical impairment are at risk of discrimination and name-calling in early years contexts. Similarly, children who are psychologically impaired through trauma like neglect or abuse, or asylum seekers, may be singled out for discrimination because of difference (Goepel et al., 2014). Social learning raises many issues around social justice, particularly in the area of gender, socio-cultural diversity and SEND. Vandenbroeck (2009) articulates concerns that often, educational contexts are contributing to social inequality, particularly for immigrant and socially challenged children.

It was noted in the previous chapter that the current UK government is committed to inclusive education and the removal of barriers to inclusion and that it is the responsibility of leaders in early years settings to achieve this goal (DfE and DoH, 2015).

> Social justice is thus not only about the enrolment of children from all social groups into preschools but also about how staff work with children from these groups within preschools in inclusive ways, countering any prejudice that might be endemic in society.
>
> (Jonsdottir and Coleman, 2014:213)

Cultural diversity

It was stated earlier in this chapter that children's development is a process which is affected by biological, social and cultural aspects. 'In this sense, culture is a medium that creates conditions for development and learning and encompasses a dynamic interaction between the child and the environment' (Williams et al., 2014:229). Children's social interactions in the early years are bound by cultural conventions and values. For example, 'cultures may differently constrain behaviours associated with cooperation, compliance or emotional expressivity' (Woolfolk and Perry, 2012:279). However, early years settings may include children from a range of ethnicities and cultural backgrounds. Siraj-Blatchford (2014) recognises that such diversity means that some children are often disadvantaged in early years education because of differences in ethnicity, gender, socio-economic class and SEND. Having a positive identity and high self-esteem may be difficult for minority groups as they are often subject to stereotyping with which they are not comfortable (Bruce, 2005, in Dowling, 2014). For example, Gypsy Roma Travellers are often perceived as being poorly educated and not fitting in with society's educational norms. Similarly, some children from particular religious backgrounds are subject to stereotypical associations with terrorism.

The enormous increase in global migration in recent years means that children who are from families who are refugees and asylum seekers arrive in the UK, often having fled war zones and extremely traumatic experiences. Refugees and asylum seekers are a diverse group who come from different cultures, speak different languages and have often come to the UK for a variety of reasons and in a range of ways. However, they are all likely to have experienced emotional upheaval, trauma through war or violence and isolation because of language difficulties and prolonged absences from schooling (Rutter, 2006; Reakes, 2007). As such, their opportunities for effective and appropriate social learning may have been limited, or even extremely negative experiences. These particular and distinctive social and emotional experiences may influence the behaviour of children who have recently arrived in the UK or who have English as an additional language (Aubrey and Ward, 2013).

A key aspect of social learning is related to communication through spoken language. However, cultural diversity in the UK is accompanied by a wide range of spoken languages in early years settings and for many children English is not their first language. The EYFS profile (STA, 2016:18) states that 'language is central to our sense of identity and belonging to a community' but recognises the value of linguistic diversity and encourages the use of home languages in early years settings. Children must be afforded opportunities to demonstrate their knowledge and understanding in their own language and their early years learning environment should reflect their linguistic and cultural heritage.

Some children may belong to travelling communities like Gypsy Roma Travellers and have different experiences of parental value attached to education. They may also have different experiences of gender roles. Research by Horgan (2007) showed that children from disadvantaged socio-economic backgrounds may not be able to afford to participate in after-school activities. Also, many boys from such backgrounds found the school day too long and the amount of work too much so that they developed a hatred of school by the time they were nine.

VIGNETTE: NEW ARRIVALS

Yasmin is six and has recently arrived in the UK. She was born in a war zone. She has spent two years in a refugee camp. After leaving the camp she spent many months travelling through Europe before arriving in the UK. Her first language is not English and she speaks very little English. She has had very little formal early years education.

■ What sort of experiences might Yasmin have had in her life?

■ How might she be affected by those experiences?

■ How may these experiences have had an impact on her social learning opportunities?

■ What sorts of activities and experiences would support her social learning in an early years setting?

Gender and social learning

The nature or nurture debate poses the question of what constitutes being male or female. Is it related to more than just physical attributes? Evolutionary psychologists like Steven Pinker believe that gender is part of our nature (Pound, 2009). Biologically girls and boys are different and there is evidence that their brains are different (Cahill, 2005, in Woolfolk and Perry, 2012). Hormones are also different in boys and girls so that male hormones tend to be more related to rough and tumble play and physical aggression. However, it is debatable whether different play behaviours among boys and girls are attributable to biological differences or the ways in which typical male/female roles have been portrayed throughout history. Hence, while biological factors are clearly significant, social factors need to be taken into consideration. Social constructivists like Rogoff (2003) believe that biological development works in tandem with cultural practices so involves both nature and nurture. For example, children learn stereotypical behaviours from observing adults and other children in their lives. So, gender development is affected by the complex interaction of biological, social and cognitive factors.

By the age of two, children normally know whether they are a boy or a girl and are aware of others being male or female. This awareness of one's own gender identity is a powerful and important aspect of self-esteem. Once children are aware of their gender identity they begin to engage in behaviours that are similar to same-sex family members and peers. They also begin to consider some activities and objects as appropriate for boys or girls and so some toys as more appropriate for girls or boys. For example, boys usually prefer playing with trucks and construction blocks while girls frequently prefer playing in the kitchen or with their dolls. They may begin establishing preferences for playing with same-sex peers and taking on stereotypical roles in role play activities. Children who do not conform to expected behaviours are often excluded or not tolerated by peers and adults (Woolfolk and Perry, 2012).

As children in the early years interact with adults, peers and siblings they observe the expected gender behaviours for their sex. These observations are further enhanced by what they see on television. For example, Grandma Pig is busily cooking potatoes for the family which Grandad Pig digs from the garden (Astley, Baker and Hall, 2004). Advertisements for a Barbie house are presented with girls playing with the house, while advertisements for construction toys are presented using boys. Children in the UK tend to be given toys that have traditionally been associated with their gender so boys receive action toys, tools and weapons while girls receive toys related to the home and care-giving. Clearly, if such stereotypical gender behaviours are encouraged by adults, children in the early years will be socialised into stereotypical behaviours in life. Boys may assume from the toys presented to them that they should use tools to do construction work or use weapons to fight. Similarly, girls assume from their toys that they should provide care, become nurses or work doing domestic chores. While all these roles and activities are important in life, it is inappropriate to 'pigeon-hole' girls and boys into stereotypes which will ultimately exclude them from certain careers or roles in life. The preponderance of such stereotypes can have an enormous impact on children's aspirations in life, their study and career choices and the roles they assume at work, home and in leisure and social situations.

Early years contexts are a prime arena for such socialisation and early years professionals need to ensure that stereotypical life-roles are not modelled in their settings. For example, it reinforces children's gendered beliefs if teachers group children by sex or compare girls' behaviour more favourably to that of boys (Woolfolk and Perry, 2012). Early years professionals are bound by the Equality Act 2010 not to discriminate against children on the basis of sex. They should provide positive learning experiences for all children, ensuring the development of positive identities and self-esteem.

So some children experience challenges in the early years because of the social effects of gender stereotyping at home and early years settings. However, some children face challenges to their social learning because they have special educational needs and/or disabilities.

Social learning and special educational needs and disability (SEND)

The government's guidance on Special Educational Needs and Disability (SEND) identifies four categories of special educational need, including 'cognition and learning', 'communication and interaction', 'sensory and physical' and 'social, emotional and mental health' (SEMH) (DfE and DoH, 2015:85). SEMH was a term introduced as a result of SEND reforms in 2014; prior to this, the term 'Behavioural, Emotional and Social Difficulties' (BESD) was used. Concerns arose around including the term 'behaviour' because defining poor behaviour is difficult and children identified with BESD were the most likely to be excluded from school (DfE, 2012).

> In many schools the opportunities for children with SEBD [social, emotional and behavioural difficulties] to make their voices heard are still very limited. Usually these are the least listened to, liked and empowered group of students ... and the most likely to be at the end of punitive and exclusionary practices.
>
> (Cefai and Cooper, 2010:184)

The change to Social Emotional and Mental Health (SEMH) needs was generally perceived as a positive way of taking away the focus on behaviour and instead exploring some of the social, emotional and mental health issues underlying behaviours. The government's current definition of SEMH is that:

Children and young people may experience a wide range of social and emotional difficulties which manifest themselves in many ways. These may include becoming withdrawn or isolated, as well as displaying challenging, disruptive or disturbing behaviour. These behaviours may reflect underlying mental health difficulties such as anxiety or depression, self-harming, substance misuse, eating disorders or physical symptoms that are medically unexplained. Other children and young people may have disorders such as attention deficit disorder, attention deficit hyperactive disorder or attachment disorder.

(DfE and DoH, 2015:98)

Aubrey and Ward (2013) argue that there is strong evidence that social and emotional difficulties are rooted in the early years. They cite Shaffer (2002), who argues that children who are socially disadvantaged and rejected by their peers are likely to have negative interactions with their peers. Children who are isolated or marginalised are likely to become aggressive and anti-social in their behaviours. Parry (2014) similarly refers to connections between unorthodox behaviours and reduced social interaction with peers. White (1996) argued that low self-esteem is at the root of many inappropriate social behaviours such as bullying and fighting. Children who feel inadequate and unable to succeed in life have a low regard for themselves and so a low self-esteem.

It is not only children with issues related to SEMH that find difficulty with social learning. Another category of SEND identified by the government is related to communication and interaction.

Children and young people with speech, language and communication needs (SLCN) have difficulty in communicating with others. This may be because they have difficulty saying what they want to, understanding what is being said to them or they do not understand or use social rules of communication. The profile for every child with SLCN is different and their needs may change over time. They may have difficulty with one, some or all of the different aspects of speech, language or social communication at different times of their lives. Children and young people with ASD, including Asperger's Syndrome and Autism, are likely to have particular difficulties with social interaction. They may also experience difficulties with language, communication and imagination, which can impact on how they relate to others.

(DfE and DoH, 2015:98)

Thus, children identified with Autistic Spectrum Disorder (ASD) display a variety of characteristics such as impaired interaction and communication with others, restricted and repetitive behaviours and interests, and delays in social interaction, social communication or symbolic or imaginative play.

Such traits, when manifested in educational settings may result in difficulties with social relations and understanding and processing information from their environment (Deris and Di Carlo, 2013). The impact of ASD on learning can be summarised as:

■ An inability to imitate sounds, gestures and gross or fine motor movements that are all necessary for learning, particularly in the early years

■ An inability to focus on the task in hand. Some have a short attention span or concentrate on one thing obsessively

■ Difficulty working collaboratively with others in class

■ Difficulty with abstract ideas, such as using items or toys to represent real objects (make-believe play and role play)

■ Difficulty grasping the concept of time and the order of events

(Peer and Reid, 2012:234)

Harbinson and Alexander (2009:18) cite issues around the English curriculum, which focuses on creativity and imaginative play so that 'To write an imaginative story … may be, not just too difficult, but perhaps impossible'.

VIGNETTE: MEETING INDIVIDUAL NEEDS

Laura is four years old and in a nursery class. Her teacher is concerned about her learning and behaviour. She has difficulties accessing the curriculum and does not respond to the teacher's instructions.

When children were asked to work in a group to construct characters with play-dough she did not interact with the other children, but played in isolation, making a snake. When asked to work in a group to create a story with the characters Laura played alone and did not engage in the task or relate to the other children. When asked to clear up she ignored the instruction.

■ What would you be concerned about if you were Laura's key person?

■ Why would you be concerned about those issues?

■ How would you have expected Laura to behave in these situations?

■ In what ways does Laura's learning and behaviour have an impact on her social learning and development?

It is clear from the above discussions and vignette that children in early years settings and contexts have wide-ranging experiences in relation to culture, gender, ethnicity, language, communication and interaction and social and emotional health. The consequence of such varied experiences may lead to challenges for social learning opportunities if equality, diversity and rights are not considered by early years practitioners. As has been stated earlier, children's social learning is influenced by the adults and children in their lives. Hence, in an increasingly global society:

> It is essential that children learn social competence to respect other groups and individuals, regardless of difference. This learning must begin in the earliest years of a child's education. Learning is thus culturally and socially influenced by the context of the child's development.
>
> (Siraj-Blatchford, 2014:181)

Conclusion

So, children's social learning in the early years is inextricably linked to other aspects of their learning. It is therefore complex and its implications are far reaching in relation to positive identity formation, self-esteem, and positive views of and respect for others. The self-assurance that children gain from collaboration enables them to speak for themselves and feel confident in solving problems and expressing their views and opinions. While some social, cultural and learning experiences might have a negative impact on children's social learning, it is the responsibility of all early years practitioners and leaders to address the varying needs of all children in order to ensure their healthy social and emotional development. This involves an awareness of a range of interactions between the child, the family, community and other stakeholders so that:

> Another influential element for inclusion in early childhood is the reciprocal relationships among child, family and community, characteristics that allow dynamic interactions between all stakeholders in early childhood education and provide the basis for understanding all involved. In that sense, inclusion should not be limited only to the development of children and their learning outcomes, but should be broadened to the social, cultural, localised contexts, where learning episodes are situated in children's behaviours and identities as learners.
>
> (Brown and Palaiologou, 2016:75)

The next chapter explores the key elements of successful leadership in the early years.

References

Ashdown, D.M. & Bernard, M.E. (2012) Can explicit instruction in social and emotional learning skills benefit the social-emotional development, well-being and academic development of young children? *Early Childhood Education Journal*, 39, 397–405.

Aubrey, C. & Ward, K. (2013) Early years practitioner's views on early personal, social and emotional development. *Emotional and Behavioural Difficulties*, 18 (4), 435–447.

Baker, W., Sammons, P., Siraj-Blatchford, I., Sylva, K., Melhuish, E.C. & Taggart, B. (2014) Aspirations, education and inequality in England: Insights from the Effective Provision of Pre-school, Primary and Secondary Education Project. *Oxford Review of Education*, 40 (5), 525–542.

Bennett, J. (2004) Curriculum issues in national policymaking. Keynote address to the EECERA Conference, Malta, September 2, 2004. Paris: Organisation for Economic Cooperation and Development.

Bronfenbrenner, U. (1979) *The Ecology of Human Development: Experiments by Nature and Design.* London: Harvard University Press.

Bronfenbrenner, U. (1986) Ecology of the family as a context for human development: Research perspectives. *Developmental Psychology*, 22 (6), 723–742.

Brown, Z. & Palaiologou, I. (2016) Inclusive practice in early childhood education. In Z. Brown (ed.), *Inclusive Education: Perspectives on Pedagogy, Policy and Practice.* Oxon: Routledge.

Bruce, T. (2005) *Early Childhood Education*, 3rd edition. London: Hodder Arnold.

Bruner, J. (1960) *The Process of Education.* Cambridge, MA: Harvard University Press.

Cahill, L. (2005) His brain, her brain. *Scientific American Magazine*, 292 (5), 40–47.

Cefai, C. & Cooper, P. (2010) Students without voices: The unheard accounts of secondary school students with social, emotional and behavioural difficulties. *European Journal of SEN*, 25 (2), 183–198.

Cunnah, W. (2012) *What Social Model? Disabled Students' Experience of Work-Related Learning and Placements.* PhD Thesis: Sheffield Hallam University.

Cunnah, W. (2015) Disabled students: Identity, inclusion and work-based placements. *Disability and Society*, 30 (2), 213–226.

Deris, A.R. & Di Carlo, C. (2013) Back to basics: Working with young children with autism in inclusive classrooms. *Support for Learning. British Journal of Learning Support*, 28 (2), 52–56.

DfE, (2012) *Pupil Behaviour in Schools in England.* London: HMSO.

DfE & DoH (2015) *Special Educational Needs and Disability Code of Practice: 0 To 25 Years.* London: HMSO. Online at: https://www.gov.uk/government/publications/send-code-of-practice-0-to-25

DfE (2017) *Statutory Framework for the Early Years Foundation Stage.* Online at: www.gov.uk/government/publications

Dowling, M. (2014) *Young Children's Personal, Social and Emotional Development*, 4th edition. London: Sage.

Elfer, P., Goldschmied, E. & Selleck, D.Y. (2012) *Key Persons in the Early Years: Building Relationships for Quality Provision in Early Years Settings and Primary Schools*, 2nd edition. Oxon: Routledge.

Equality Act 2010 Guidance (2015) Online at: https://www.gov.uk/guidance/equality-act-2010-guidance

Gardner, H. (1986) *Emotional Intelligence.* London: Bloomsbury.

Gardner, H. (1993) *Frames of Mind*, 2nd edition. London: Fontana.

Goepel, J., Childerhouse, H. & Sharpe, S. (2014) *Inclusive Primary Teaching: A Critical Approach to Equality and Special Educational Needs.* Northwich: Critical Publishing.

Harbinson, H. & Alexander, J. (2009) Asperger syndrome and the English curriculum: Addressing the challenges. *Support for Learning*, 24 (1), 11–18.

Horgan, G. (2007) *The Impact of Poverty on Young People's Experiences of School.* Joseph Rowntree Foundation. Online at: http://learning.gov.wales/docs/learningwales/publications/120817experienceen.pdf

Jenkins, R. (2004) *Social Identity*, 2nd edition. London: Routledge.

Jonsdottir, A.H. & Coleman, M. (2014) Professional role identity of Icelandic preschool teachers: Effects of stakeholders' views. *Early Years*, 34 (3), 210–225.

Langford, R. (2010) Critiquing child-centred pedagogy to bring children and early childhood educators into the centre of democratic pedagogy. *Contemporary Issues in Early Childhood*, 11 (1), 113–127.

Lebedeva, G. (2015) Building brains one relationship at a time. *Exchange*, 11, Nov/Dec 2015, 21–25.

Lindon, J. (2005) *Understanding Child Development: Linking Theory and Practice.* London: Hodder Education.

Parry, J. (2014) Making connections and making friends: Social interactions between two children labelled with special educational needs and their peers in a nursery setting. *Early Years*, 34 (3), 310–314.

Peer, L. & Reid, G. (2012) *Special Educational Needs: A Guide for Inclusive Practice.* London: Sage.

Pound, L. (2008) *How Children Learn: From Montessori to Vygotsky.* London: Practical Pre-School Books.

Pound, L. (2009) *How Children Learn 3: Contemporary Thinking and Theorists.* London: Practical Pre-School Books.

Reakes, A. (2007) The education of asylum seekers: Some UK case studies. *Research in Education*, 77, 92–107. Swansea: NFER.

Rogoff, B. (2003) *The Cultural Nature of Human Development.* Oxford: Oxford University Press.

Rutter, J. (2006) *Refugee Children in the United Kingdom.* Maidenhead: OU Press.

Siraj-Blatchford, I. (2014) Diversity, inclusion and learning in the early years. In G. Pugh & B. Duffy (eds), *Contemporary Issues in the Early Years*, 6th edition. London: Sage.

Shaffer, D. R. (2002) *Developmental Psychology*, 6th edition. Oxford: Blackwell.

Standards and Testing Agency (STA) (2016) *Early Years Foundation Stage Profile: 2017 Handbook.* Online at: https://www.gov.uk/government/uploads/system/uploads/attachment_data/file/564249/2017_EYFSP_handbook_v1.1.pdf

Swain, J. & French, S. (2008) *Disability on Equal Terms.* London: Sage.

Vandenbroeck, M. (2009) Let us disagree. *European Early Childhood Education Research Journal*, 17, (2) 165–170.

White, M. (1996) What's so silly about self-esteem? *TES*, 26 April, p.3.

Williams, P., Sheridan, S. & Sandberg, A. (2014) Preschool – an arena for children's learning of social and cognitive knowledge. *Early Years*, 34, (3), 226–240.

Woodward, K., (2000) Questions of identity. In K. Woodward (ed.), *Questioning Identity: Gender, Class, Nation.* London: Routledge.

Woolfolk, A. & Perry, N.E. (2012) *Child and Adolescent Development.* Pearson: New Jersey.

6 Leadership for learning

Introduction

In Chapter 2 we emphasised the need for highly reflective leaders. We looked at some national frameworks and considered how these helped leaders to conceptualise their work. Thinking leaders are needed to critique and adapt these frameworks to fit their specific contexts. In Chapter 3 we said that practitioners need knowledge and understanding about emotional development in order to support children in their play and think about appropriate interventions. Reflective practitioners are needed to offer respectful guidance to parents, and provide learning experiences that allow every child to feel positive about their learning. In Chapter 4 we said leaders had responsibility for achieving successful inclusion. Early years leaders must have high expectations for all children, including those with special educational needs or disabilities. In Chapter 5 we looked at some challenges faced by early years practitioners when implementing social learning, particularly in diverse socio-cultural contexts and with children for whom social learning is challenging. Skilled and knowledgeable leaders are needed to motivate and guide their teams through this complex work with very young children and families.

In this chapter we consider what sorts of people are needed for this broad and intricate work in early years. What does research say about leadership? What are some of the specific dilemmas and issues that early years leaders face? What sorts of leaders are needed in a rapidly changing, highly digitised world? What sorts of leaders are needed for the future? This chapter attempts to explore these questions.

Effective early years leadership

Strong leadership is essential in the early years, especially to support young children's healthy emotional, sensory and social learning. The word 'strong', however, does not imply a tough, hard or detached approach. Strong leadership in this context goes hand in hand with sensitivity, self-knowledge, reflection and imagination. Leaders with these qualities have a clear vision, but remain flexible and open to change. They communicate well with children, families and colleagues, as well as with local and regional leaders within the field of early years and from other disciplines. These sensitive and skilled leaders are committed to collaboration.

Aubrey (2010) emphasised the importance of strong collaboration in the early years. Early years leaders 'collaborate across the community to provide joined-up high quality services for babies, children and families' (Aubrey, 2010:221). A joined-up approach is necessary to support healthy emotional, sensory and social learning in the early years. Leaders need to connect with relevant bodies to support individual children and model healthy, positive relationships in their work.

Teams under strong leadership communicate well and are committed to their work with young children and families. Strong, sensitive leaders establish trust within teams. They build resilience in the face of continuous change. In this chapter we construct effective early years leaders as

1 Excellent communicators

2 Trusting of their teams

3 Highly reflective

4 Open to change, viewing it as an opportunity for learning and growth, and

5 Committed to helping children develop well through their emotions, senses and social encounters

Early years leaders to navigate changing political landscapes

Early years leaders work within an ever-changing political landscape in England. Policies change with every new government. The Labour government (1997–2010), for example, invested a lot of money in the early years. It launched the Sure Start programme in 1998 to give children the best possible start in life through quality childcare, early education, health and family support. In 2003 it introduced the Every Child Matters policy. The main aims of the policy were for every child, whatever their background or circumstances, to have the support they need to:

1 Stay safe

2 Be healthy

3 Enjoy and achieve

4 Make a positive contribution, and

5 Achieve economic well-being

There was an emphasis on multi-agency partnerships so that leaders worked together to achieve these outcomes. The aim was for different professionals to adopt a joined-up approach to their work so as to reduce unnecessary repetition and ensure that the needs of every child were fully met. The Conservative/Liberal Democrat coalition government (2010–2015) that followed the Labour government promoted the notion of 'school readiness' (DfE, 2014). The government was concerned that children did not make rapid enough progress and suggested that this was because many settings passed on unreliable assessments. Accordingly, the coalition government promoted such practices as baseline assessments for younger children in school. This government reduced the expansive, principled framework launched by the previous government to a slim, more subject-focused document. It introduced a phonics test in 2015, whereby children aged 5 and 6 must read pseudo-words, e.g. 'jigh', 'rird', 'phope'.

It could be argued that keeping up with international league tables was the political driver behind these moves, and 'school readiness' the lever through which parents and other parties were persuaded that these developments were positive. In any case, regardless of whether or not a phonetic approach to teaching reading suits some children, professionals and researchers (Rose, 2009) agree that this is not the case for all children.

New statutory frameworks and non-statutory guidance materials are launched by successive political parties, and new governance, funding and regulatory systems replace old ones along similar forward and backward trajectories. This aspect of ongoing change poses both a challenge and an opportunity for early years leaders. It is challenging in the sense that leaders need to draw up new setting policies to meet new government requirements, provide appropriate training and change their systems as necessary. It is an opportunity in the sense that teams are inevitably brought together to reflect on their practices and systems. For example, when teaching children reading through phonics became enshrined in law (DfES, 2007), teachers and other people involved in the teaching of reading needed to balance what they understood as important for early literacy development with new policy requirements. Inevitably this led to talk about people's professional understanding of the topic, and how people could marry up their principles with new policies. If they believed that a range of approaches was needed to support early reading, for example, how could they continue to offer this while meeting the new government requirements for daily phonics sessions? People engaged in professional talk.

We suggest that effective early years leaders are needed to facilitate such discussions and make decisions. Such leaders are able to build up strong, flexible teams made up of people who welcome change and are mutually supportive and understanding of each other in turbulent times. Elfer and Page (2015:1778) found that when strong leaders embraced uncertainty and had 'the courage to reflect openly' with others, their organisations appeared strengthened as well. Strong leaders, from these perspectives, support teams to navigate their way through successive new requirements. This is difficult work.

In the 2016 White Paper 'Educational Excellence Everywhere', the Department for Education in England made a connection between school leadership and the quality of education a child receives. The message the government put forward was that highly effective leaders make a positive impact in the setting where they work and raise the achievement of children. The government set out to widen the impact of effective leadership by directing strong leaders to where they were most needed. The driver behind this paper was to raise standards and improve outcomes for children. Strong leaders were needed not only to support individual children to develop and learn, but to drive up standards more broadly. Leaders would be held 'to account' (DfE, 2016:40) if outcomes were not good.

To achieve this 'educational excellence everywhere', the government wanted strong leaders across the breadth of the country and, in particular, in challenging areas. Accordingly, the government expressed a commitment to train more high quality leaders and create more opportunities for them to work in the areas where they would create the most difference. The government wanted to create 'a strong and sustainable pipeline of talented, motivated leaders working in challenging areas' (DfE, 2016:40). This was a big ambition to drive up outcomes across all areas of the country.

And yet, government resources for training early years leaders in England have been gradually eroded. The acclaimed National Professional Qualification for Integrated Centre Leadership programme, for example, no longer operates. Additionally, despite recommendations from a national review of qualifications (Nutbrown, 2013) and report about the quality of early childhood education and care for children under three (Mathers et al., 2014) that a highly qualified, graduate-led workforce was needed in early years, no legislation is yet in place to support this ambition.

In this section we considered how early years leaders in England work in a continually changing political landscape. We talked about the challenges this posed but also emphasised the increased opportunities for professional talk. In the next section we consider what sort of leaders are needed for the complex work involved in early years.

Leaders for complex work

The work of early years leaders in relation to children's emotional, sensory and social learning is highly complex. As has been explored in other chapters in this book, young children need to feel cherished and experience closeness. In Chapter 1, we suggested that young children's earliest emotional and sensory experiences shape their brain architecture for life (Lebedeva, 2015) and contribute to who they become as older children, and as adults. Drawing on Dowling (2010), we emphasised the importance of helping children to build up a bank of happy memories to nourish them throughout life, and to draw on in difficult times. In Chapter 2 we suggested that there are no simple explanations about how children learn. We constructed the world as messy and in flux, with multiple challenges and possible interpretations, and no clear solutions. In Chapter 3, we argued that children need love and emphasised the importance of establishing loving encounters in the workplace. Early years professionals, as Noddings (2007:223) proposed, need to consider how to respond to each child as if they were a member of their family, or 'inner circle'. In Chapters 4 and 5 we explored the notion of inclusion and suggested that the responsibility for achieving inclusive practice lay with early years leaders. Early years leaders carry significant responsibility for the health, education and social, emotional well-being of all children in their care.

Early years practitioners face issues and dilemmas in relation to affective matters of their work. For example, practitioners need to consider whether close and intimate relationships are appropriate in non-familial contexts, whether it is advisable for them to show children they are loved through the expression of touch, or how they should address parental concerns in different areas. Some leaders may adopt the view that settings provide a very different sort of experience for children, and that a familial style of love is inappropriate in their settings.

Accordingly, they may seek to prevent any possible allegations against members of staff by establishing highly restrictive policies in respect of how adults are allowed to communicate affection to children.

REFLECTION: APPROPRIATE TOUCH

■ How do leaders at your setting support you to build up children's self-esteem and healthy emotional, social development?

■ What do policies at your setting say about appropriate touch with children?

Having explored some of the dilemmas faced by leaders in early years contexts, particularly in relation to affective matters between adults and children. We now consider the issue of touch and the need to make difficult decisions that are both beneficial for children and attentive to what might go wrong.

Leaders to decide how adults should show children they are loved

The subject of touching young children is a dilemma that early years practitioners face. In recent years touch has become linked with paedophilia in England and is sometimes perceived as sexual. We argue that this is rarely the case. Owen and Gillentine (2011) highlighted the importance of touching children as a means of communicating love. They outlined cultural barriers that stand in the way of this ethical approach. For example, they talked about fear and moral panic related to child abuse allegations. They pointed to a wide gap between what professionals believe to be right, namely that touch is important, and what they are able to put into practice in the light of possible negative repercussions.

Early years practitioners in England work within a wider cultural context of fear in which, according to Sikes and Piper (2010:20), adults are sometimes regarded with suspicion, as if they may be 'sexual predators' and children as sexual victims. Early years practitioners, suggested Sikes and Piper, may not always feel able to enter into loving exchanges with children that involve touch since 'for a professional adopting the status of *in loco parentis* is a dangerous thing to do' (Sikes and Piper, 2010:22). Early years leaders play an important role in supporting teams in the face of these dilemmas.

So, on the one hand it is argued that touch is important for young children's emotional development (Noddings, 2001, 2007; Gerhardt, 2004; Manning-Morton, 2006; Owen and Gillentine, 2011), and on the other hand, some researchers (Piper and Smith, 2003; Sikes and Piper, 2010) argue that any form of physical contact between adults and children is dangerous. Early years leaders need to be clear about where they stand in relation to this issue so that they can provide encouragement, direction and support as needed. Is it or is it not right for practitioners to show love to children through the expression of touch? Leaders need to adopt a clear stance in relation to this aspect of emotional, sensory and social learning.

Powell and Goouch (2012) emphasised a professional conflict of interests in relation to safety in baby rooms. Participants in their Baby Room study said it was important to love children in their care. They also said that worries about child protection shaped their day-to-day approach with the children. In other words, these practitioners did not feel able to show the children that they were loved through expressions of touch.

It is not appropriate for leaders to avoid this tricky issue and simply establish stringent policies, for example whereby teams are not allowed to put children on their laps when they need comfort, or cuddle them when they awake from their sleep. If touch becomes too restricted, calculated or controlled in early years contexts, Piper and Smith (2003) argued, it could lose some of its positive effects and risk becoming dangerously sterile, overly safe and sanitised. Restrictive policies in relation to touch, Piper and Smith suggested, while established to protect adults and children, offer an impoverished experience for children; they recommended a more flexible stance with opportunities for practitioners to talk about fears and explore contradictions. Sensitive and astute leaders are needed to establish these opportunities.

> **VIGNETTE:** SHOWING LOVE TO CHILDREN
>
> How does Jordan, deputy manager at a private, voluntary and independent setting, navigate what she considers natural ways to show children they are loved and setting policies and norms?
>
> 'This is quite a difficult thing to answer. I feel as though it is all about finding the balance between right and wrong. After all, we are not their parents but we do still feel love towards children and have a natural instinct to love and protect them.
>
> I am lucky enough to work within a setting that promotes a homely atmosphere and the love of a child. My setting does not have policies that restrict things such as cuddles or sitting on adults' laps, etc. ..., although this cannot be said for some other settings. However, it does still safeguard the children, through our safeguarding and whistleblowing policies and procedures.
>
> I am not a parent but I am aware through my own private work and educational experiences that children need love and affection in order to flourish and develop appropriately. Physical touch, such as cuddles, a pat on the back, a rub on the cheek, etc. ... are all necessary, especially for babies.

I know the limits and I know the difference between what is right and wrong. This helps my colleagues and me to balance out how much love to show towards a child.

Whilst a child is within the setting, we are their main carers. We are the people children turn to for love and comfort. Therefore, as long as the restrictions and boundaries are made clear within a setting, who are we to restrict a child from love?

Balance and clear boundaries are key in ensuring children are shown love and affection in an appropriate way. It is also important that all practitioners in a setting are aware of the safeguarding boundaries and never overstep them. A clear understanding of what love and affection mean and what they mean for a child are also key.'

■ How does Jordan know what is appropriate in relation to showing children they are loved through expressions of touch?

■ What helps Jordan and her colleagues to feel confident in this area?

Cultural fears about touching children limit what professionals can do. For example, as explored in Chapter 3, practitioners in the Baby Room research project felt restricted about showing children affection. The research by Goouch and Powell (2013) showed that any constraints on what practitioners felt they could do, related to cultural concerns around child protection issues, affected the quality of care they provided. As we have argued, since children need to feel loved, this is not a desirable situation.

To summarise, early years leaders must draw up appropriate safeguarding policies, and yet policies can be over-restrictive. Such over-restrictive policies in relation to touch may inhibit the intuitive side of people's professionalism and create a tension between what they consider privately, as ethical people, and what they are prescribed to do as public professionals (Cousins, 2015). The issue of touch, then, adds complexity of the role of early years leaders, particularly in supporting children's healthy emotional and social development. In the next section we emphasise the value of professional talk and discuss how leaders can facilitate this.

Leaders to establish time for talk within teams

We have argued that there is a need for an acute awareness about the complexity of the work, particularly in the area of close relationships with children. It may be that some practitioners, for example, establish loving relationships with some children, feel sad when they leave their care, feel unable to talk about this in the workplace, or feel inhibited about touching children to show them that they are loved.

One form of support is for leaders to provide opportunities for practitioners to reflect on their own practice. Manning-Morton (2006:48) emphasised the importance of practitioners developing as mature, emotionally intelligent, self-aware adults, and 'becom[ing] experts in themselves'. She recommended that leaders offer support to their teams to help them meet day-to-day challenges, including instances when they may be rejected by children. Manning-Morton emphasised that work with very young children involves practitioners' hearts as much as their minds.

Similarly, Osgood (2011:131) argued that practitioners need 'improved support' in order to mitigate the human cost of this 'emotionally demanding work'. Osgood (2011:130) proposed that leaders should encourage practitioners to draw on their 'life experience and wisdom', as indicated within her concept of 'professionalism from within', so that they might develop an even 'deeper-level appreciation for the work (i.e. professionalism)'. The complexity of the role was also emphasised by Harwood et al. (2013). They found, in their international study, that love was very important in practitioners' constructions about professionalism in early years, and proposed that leaders provide more opportunities for practitioners to talk about the emotional aspects of their roles.

Page and Elfer (2013:564) found that practitioners sometimes relied on their intuition or simply translated their own experiences of being in close relationships to their nursery contexts, and proposed, instead, that there should be a clear distinction between close and intimate relationships experienced in the family and in early years settings. They found that staff often adopted 'a largely intuitive approach' in relation to their work, 'drawing on personal experience rather than a body of theoretical knowledge'. As discussed in Chapter 3, they argued that leaders should create opportunities for staff to discuss complex issues around their work, and allow safe and open debates. Hence, Page and Elfer (2013) proposed that leaders should establish a climate whereby practitioners can feel free to discuss sensitive matters in an open and honest manner. This accords with the theoretical stances outlined in Chapter 2, whereby practitioners accept uncertainty and contradictions, especially in relation to affective aspects of their work.

As discussed in Chapter 2, Goouch and Powell (2013:83) found that the baby room practitioners were very willing to engage in their Baby Room project and learn from each other. The 'critical spaces' they established for talking and thinking helped practitioners 'to develop a sense of their own worth in their work and to develop a "voice" (2013:87). 'Time for talk' (2013:84) helped them to think about their practice and gain a better understanding about their work. Opportunities for 'professional talk' (2013:83), according to Goouch and Powell, helped the participants in their research to interpret their experiences in the baby room, value particular aspects of their work, make links with their own life experiences, reflect, think about their practice, and consider other possibilities. 'Talk through narrative constructions' (2013:85), they found, was a powerful learning experience.

VIGNETTE: TIME TO TALK ABOUT ISSUES

A child found it difficult to settle at the nursery. She arrived with her mother every day but clung onto her when it was time for her mother to go. The key person learned how to say 'Mummy is coming back' in the child's home language, Polish, and sang the refrain repeatedly and soothingly. The key person remained with the child for extended periods every morning, and comforted her with her constant presence, gestures and facial expressions, but the child continued to show signs of distress. The team talked with each other about the situation and how it made them feel. They talked in passing, informally at the end of the day and at formal team meetings. They explored different strategies, drawing on their different perspectives and experiences with other children. These opportunities for talk served to reduce their tension about the issue, share any sense of responsibility and focus on solutions. Talk helped them to feel they were not alone. After a period the child came to nursery happily and parted from her mother with ease.

- How did practitioners help the child to settle at nursery?

- What helped the key person to develop strategies and feel supported?

In this section we talked about the complexity of the role of early years practitioners. We said that on the one hand it is important to form close relationships with children in early years contexts, while on the other, this carries complexities, often unspoken and unacknowledged. Osgood (2011) called for more space to be made for people to draw on their subjective experiences to enhance their professional practice. Goouch and Powell (2013) emphasised the value of talk. In the next section we consider some large-scale research findings on the topic of leadership. What does research say about quality leadership?

Leadership qualities – some findings from big research

Matthews et al. (2014) carried out research for the National College of Teaching and Leadership. They identified the conditions that must lie behind such successful outcomes in the early years. These optimum conditions included consistently good teaching, a stimulating and well-designed curriculum, a culture of empowering children to become capable and self-aware learners, high expectations and close attention to the needs of individual children (Matthews et al., 2014:18).

The researchers set out to find out what sort of people effective leaders were, what they did, how they did it and how they capitalised on national and local policies for education. They found that strong leaders were driven by a commitment to do the best for every child. Children remained at the heart of everything they did. These committed leaders also had a strong sense of social justice, seeking to remove barriers to achievement, such as disadvantage and low parental aspirations. Matthews et al. (2014) found that leaders committed to social justice developed close links with families and communities, and were able to address any gaps children had and make up the difference.

Strong leaders, Matthews et al. (2014) found, maintained a single-minded focus on teaching and learning, in order to maximise the achievement of all. From a sample of fifty primary school leaders in 2013, Matthews et al. (2014) found that effective leaders were:

- Resilient

- Passionate

- Focused

- Visionary and inspiring

- Clear and communicative

- Relentless and tenacious

- Reflective

- Courageous

- Challenging, with high expectations

They found that these leaders were motivated and driven by their desire to do well for children. They also had attributes associated with moral purpose, including:

- Honesty

- Openness

- Emotional intelligence

- Belief

Matthews et al. found that leaders were good at problem solving and willing to take risks. They were energetic, engaged, organised, encouraging and motivating.

REFLECTION: LEADERSHIP QUALITIES

- Why might it be important for leaders to be honest, open and emotionally intelligent?

- What other qualities do leaders need to support children in the early years?

- How do effective leaders in your workplace help children to feel happy and be ready to grow as caring, strong individuals?

- What are leaders' responsibilities in relation to legislation? How do they incorporate the Code of Practice for Special Educational Needs and Disabilities (DfE and DoH, 2015)?

The researchers found that good leaders focused all their actions on the effect they would have on children and their learning. Importantly, they were strong communicators. They consulted with colleagues and were determined to lead by example. Crucially, good leaders trusted their teams. They knew when to take control and when to delegate. At the same time, however, they never let go completely. They took risks, did not ascribe blame and always looked for the positive in others and in different situations.

Good leaders, Matthews et al. (2014) found, led by example and respected each individual. They faced up to difficult conversations or hard decisions. They trusted colleagues and empowered them to develop their own careers. In settings run by effective leaders, researchers found that staff felt trusted to lead, innovate, experiment and take risks. Indeed, they were encouraged to do so. Additionally, children were also encouraged to lead, to learn with and from their peers, and to take responsibility for their learning – seeking out and rising to new or harder challenges.

Outstanding leaders, they found, had a propensity for seizing new opportunities. Rather than being dominated by external ideologies, they were driven by their beliefs and values. They built up structures and cultures which took account of national policies but which remained in line with identified improvement priorities. Importantly, these researchers concluded that leaders with vision took advantage of the opportunities presented, not in order to enhance their reputation or career prospects, but for the benefit of the children in their care.

So, in contrast to the political focus on outcomes, effective leaders work according to a strong ethical code. They want the best for the children and families in their care, and motivate their teams to work with them towards the same goals.

In this section we explored what research shows in relation to quality leadership. In the next section we turn to practice, and consider how these findings can support people's work with very young children and their families.

From big research to local practice

How can these findings from large-scale research support leadership for emotional, sensory and social learning in the early years? As Matthews et al. (2014) found, effective leaders have a commitment to do the best for every child. Accordingly, they attend closely to children's social and emotional needs. They establish close relationships with children. They support them in a range of social contexts to grow as self-confident, considerate and aware human beings, able to negotiate meanings with others and express their creativity with confidence. Good leaders lead by example, so are able to model the excellent dispositions and qualities they foster in their teams. They trust their colleagues to be people of feeling, self-aware, with a strong sense of what is right and just. Good leaders encourage children to take the lead and take responsibility for their learning. For example, a good leader will plan unhurried opportunities for teams to talk about new policies and practices rather than impose them without consultation. Similarly, they will induct new staff members slowly, allowing them to shadow an experienced key person over time, and ask questions about their practice in relation to particular children.

Having considered how big research might relate to different work contexts, we now introduce the notion of emotional labour and how this can help us to frame thinking about leadership in early years.

Leaders for work that involves emotional labour

Hochschild's (2002) notion of emotional labour was developed in the 1980s. The research related to studies of air-hostesses. Hochschild wrote about the negative aspects of working with the emotions. Air-hostesses felt drained after a day of being nice to strangers, and were unable to switch off easily. For Hochschild, emotional labour was about emotion management within the workplace. So, in cases where employees are required to enact a particular emotional state, they need to deny what they really feel, and this is difficult.

Similarly, the work that early years practitioners do 'calls for coordination of mind and feeling' (Hochschild, 2002:194). Early years practitioners call on their emotions as part of their work. For example, they enter into relationships with the children they care for. However, a more positive understanding has emerged in relation to emotional labour (Lynch, Baker and Lyons, 2009), as well as in the context of early years (Boyer, Reimer and Irvine, 2012), and we will now discuss these perspectives.

Lynch et al. (2009:45) wrote about 'love labour' instead of emotional labour. They argued that love labour, like emotional labour, 'involves physical and mental work as well as emotional work'. They also emphasised that their conceptualisation of care work as love labour incorporated both the negative and positive aspects of the work. They wrote that, although love labour may be heavy at times, it was also 'pure pleasure'.

Boyer et al. (2012:529), too, identified positive feelings in relation to early years practitioners' 'emotional investments' with children. Some of the practitioner leaders in five nurseries where they conducted their research said that the fact they could develop close relationships with children was a feature they liked about their role. The research showed that developing 'emotional bonds' (2012:535) with children in nurseries could be rewarding and 'deeply gratifying'. Accordingly, the authors argued that the affective work carried out by early years practitioners was not the same as the 'emotional labour associated with other forms of waged care work' (2012:525).

Cousins (2017), in her small-scale research about love in out-of-home contexts, found that practitioners liked the emotional aspect of their work. Yes, they may have admitted that they felt sad when certain children left their settings, or faced dilemmas, for example when children expressed a desire, in front of their parents, to remain in their company at the end of the day. However, participants in Cousins' research said that they loved their work despite such difficulties. Their work could be classified as emotional labour, but the pleasures of doing it far outweighed any emotional costs.

Accordingly, we support the view that presents emotional labour in a positive frame (Lynch et al., 2009; Boyer et al., 2012; Cousins, 2017). These different understandings of emotional labour, however, from undesirable and burdensome at one end of the continuum to desirable and pleasurable at the other, are also helpful, in our view, in that they serve to remind us of the intensely personal nature of work in early years.

Early years leaders, as opposed to practitioners, including teachers, nursery nurses, learning support assistants, classroom assistants, sole childminders and others, enter a further layer of emotional space. Not only does work with very young children carry complexities and dilemmas, as has been discussed, but the leadership role itself establishes new dimensions and creates potential tensions. Mitchell, Riley and Loughran (2010:543) proposed that there are emotional dimensions to leadership, as well as tensions associated with leading colleagues. They suggested that leadership is at once 'a deeply personal experience' as well as highly complex work. In their research, educational leaders talked about the emotional, personal and relational components of leading colleagues in diverse contexts, particularly in the area of professional learning. Leaders used emotional language to talk about their work as leaders. They said they felt anxiety, frustration, elation, despair, confidence and relief. Leaders also admitted to feeling vulnerable at times. Responses from team members to their professional learning initiatives affected their own emotions as people and leaders.

According to Mitchell et al. (2010), then, there are additional emotional costs to being a leader. Educational leaders engage in emotional labour. Not only is teaching and learning highly relational work, so is their own work as leaders of teams. Leaders talk about 'the intensity of feeling when working with colleagues while assuming leadership responsibilities' (Mitchell et al., 2010:540).

John (2008: 64) explored the advantages of mentoring for leaders. According to John, mentoring opportunities for leaders open up spaces where leaders feel cared for both as professionals and people. When leaders are well mentored and cared for, they can take time to explore particularly complex aspects of their work, for example aspects relating to working with children, families and other professionals in an integrated way. Mentoring opportunities, John found, helped leaders feel 'valued, respected and encouraged'. These feelings, in turn, can help leaders to support the people they serve to feel valued, respected and encouraged.

In this section we explored the notion of emotional labour and suggested that, in early years contexts, this aspect of people's work is often what they like about it. Although the emotional side of the work may be difficult, or even painful, at times, it is more frequently pleasurable. People talk about it in teams. We now explore research that suggests leaders might benefit from reflecting on their own life experiences alongside their complex work.

Leadership dispositions – some findings from small, qualitative research

The best leaders are outstanding people and professionals. They do not emerge in the field of early childhood by good luck or accident, but by hard work, commitment, passion and determination. The best leaders have a strong moral purpose. It is true that some people may be 'natural' leaders, but this in itself does not imply that they will be effective as early years leaders. On the contrary, strong leaders develop their skills over time, through training, learning in the workplace, strong teamwork and reflection. Strong leaders are also highly intuitive and in touch with themselves as people. They are self-aware, and have done some work on themselves.

Layen (2015), in her in-depth study of early years leaders, found that leaders gained much by relating their work to their personal life stories. She discovered that when leaders reflect on their personal autobiographies, in the form of narrated life stories, their self-concept, self-awareness and self-belief were enhanced. When leaders made links between personal and leadership narratives, Layen found, they developed a clearer vision and a clearer moral purpose, and became more motivated.

Leaders' own emotional stories, from this perspective, play a part in how well they are able to support children's emotional development. Leaders' own sensitivities for the arts, for example, affect the extent to which they prioritise the arts in their settings. Their ability to communicate effectively with the teams and communities they serve also help children to develop strong social skills. Children benefit from sensitive, emotionally resilient and socially competent leaders. There is a correlation between these skills and sensitivities in early years leaders and the opportunities available to children in relation to their emotional, sensory and social learning.

We have considered a range of skills and characteristics associated with the role of leadership. We now explore the sorts of leaders that might be needed for the future.

Leadership for the future

As the world evolves and new policies emerge on the early years landscape, so new pressures and priorities become more prominent for leaders of early years settings. Advances in digital technologies, for example, open up new opportunities as well as create challenges for early years leaders and the children and families they serve. Leaders need to consider how technologies might support children in their learning. For example, how can assistive technologies help children with special educational needs and disabilities in their learning? How can tablets help children to develop their literacy skills? At the same time, leaders face new challenges in relation to digital advances. They must consider ways to ensure their children remain safe in online environments. Leaders need to begin from the premise that online predators and child exploiters roam freely. To this end, they must consider a range of potential dangers. For example, should parents and carers be allowed to take pictures of their children at school celebrations? Similarly, should children be allowed to use mobile technology at the setting? Should leaders block out the outside world to keep children safe? Conversely, should they help children to recognise danger, understand the need to avoid it and know how to remain safe?

VIGNETTE: TEACHING CHILDREN TO STAY SAFE IN ONLINE ENVIRONMENTS

Donna, a teaching assistant in a Year 1 class at a primary school, shares her approach to teaching children about online safety. Consider how effective such a strategy might be in your context.

'It can be a challenge to discuss the topic of online safety with five- and six-year-olds without raising panic and alarm, or causing anxiety. In accordance with the school's e-safety policy, circle time sessions serve as opportunities to teach children how to stay safe online.

At a recent circle time I led, I began by asking the children what technology they had at home and whether they used the internet. I then asked the children if they knew what to do if they saw something that upset them or made them feel uncomfortable. They responded with phrases such as "Tell a teacher" and "Tell my mum". We went on to discuss what to do if they were worried about something they had seen on the internet.

I used puppets to discuss and emphasise the importance of staying safe. We discussed the importance of not sharing any personal information such as names and addresses, and of only using the internet with an adult's permission and when a grown-up was nearby. We discussed how important it was not to download anything without permission from an adult. Finally, I sought confirmation from every child that they had a safe person they could talk to if they were worried about anything they had seen or used on the internet.

A child ended the session with the comment "I would tell my mummy and she would call the policeman and he would take the bad iPad man away because he's a stranger danger".

- How do you keep children safe online?

- What sorts of issues do you face in relation to online safety?

Inevitably, new priorities and potential hazards create new opportunities for ongoing training and development. What sorts of knowledge and skills must early years teams have? How can leaders help their teams to meet the relevant professional standards in ever-changing contexts?

In this book we have emphasised the importance of research. Research about brain architecture, for example, informs new guidance on early emotional, sensory and social learning. Sensitive, attuned interactions between key adults and children, for example, are key for healthy brain development. Accordingly, we suggest that leaders for the future are research informed. It is not enough, we propose, that leaders study child development as part of their initial training. Rather, it is desirable that they perceive themselves as lifelong learners, with always more to learn. Leaders in the future are future proof. They make it their business to find out what is happening, remain informed about new research, discuss possibilities with their teams and effect change as needed.

Perhaps, however, it is the enduring people-to-people qualities in settings that help children thrive in difficult situations. This description of practice from 1946 about support for children who had lived through the Second World War remains relevant today:

> Teachers save children from the stresses and strains of their early life through their daily relations with children and through the kind of experiences they make it possible for children to have in the daily school program. Sensitive teachers have long done it. They start with a faith in children and with a conviction that all children want to be good if they can. They know in their hearts that, when something goes wrong, there is a reason why. With these attitudes to build on, teachers have found their own ways to make their schools friendly places. They have worked so that children, each and every one of them, get *in* and belong.
>
> (Hymes, 1946:191)

So, sensitivity and close relationships between adults and children are at the heart of effective practice. Leaders must build places where children feel valued by the people who care for them, and are nurtured through whatever difficulties they may encounter or experience.

Conclusion

In Chapter 2 we argued that a pragmatic, postmodern stance might be a helpful position to adopt in order to counter-balance the current emphasis on pre-specified goals, certain outcomes and strict accountability. We said that the world is uncertain and unpredictable, and that a flexible approach was therefore needed to navigate ongoing change. In this chapter we have suggested that knowledgeable, sensitive and intuitive early years leaders are needed for this highly complex work set in ever-shifting contexts. Effective early year leaders communicate well with their teams and foster a culture where there is time for talk, team members feel encouraged to explore difficult options, and parents and children contribute to the decision-making process. These leaders value creativity and openness in the context of careful planning and self-evaluation.

References

Aubrey, C. (2010) Leading and working in multi-agency teams. In G. Pugh & B. Duffy (eds), *Contemporary Issues in the Early Years*, 5th edition. London, Sage.

Boyer, K., Reimer, S. & Irvine, L. (2012) The nursery workspace, emotional labour and contested understandings of commoditized childcare in the contemporary UK. *Social and Cultural Geography*, 14 (5), 517–540.

Cousins, S. (2015) *Practitioners' Constructions of Love in the Context of Early Childhood Education and Care: A Narrative Inquiry* (Unpublished EdD research thesis, University of Sheffield, Sheffield). Online at: http://etheses.whiterose.ac.uk/8855/

Cousins, S. (2017) Practitioners' constructions of love in early childhood education and care. *International Journal of Early Years Education*, 25 (1), 16–29.

Department for Education (DfE) (2014) *Are You Ready? Good Practice in School-Readiness.* Online at: https://www.gov.uk/government/publications/are-you-ready-good-practice-in-school-readiness

Department for Education (DfE) (2016) *Educational Excellence Everywhere.* Online at: www.gov.uk/government/publications

Department for Education and Department of Health (DfE and DoH) (2015) *Special Educational Needs and Disability Code of Practice: 0–25 Years.* Online at: https://www.gov.uk/government/uploads/system/uploads/attachment_data/file/398815/SEND_Code_of_Practice_January_2015.pdf

Department for Education and Skills (DfES) (2007) *Letters and Sounds: Principles and Practice of High Quality Phonics.*

Dowling, M. (2010) Strength of feeling. *Nursery World* (Haymarket Business Publications Ltd). 3/11/2010, 110 (4210), p. 14–16. Online at www.nurseryworld.co.uk

Elfer, P. (2012) Emotion in nursery work: Work discussion as a model of critical professional reflection. *Early Years*, 32 (2), 129–141.

Elfer, P. & Page, J. (2015) Pedagogy with babies: Perspectives of eight nursery managers. *Early Child Development and Care*, 185 (11–12), 1762–1782.

Gerhardt, S. (2004) *Why Love Matters: How Affection Shapes a Baby's Brain.* London: Routledge.

Goouch, K. & Powell, S. (2013) Orchestrating professional development for baby room practitioners: Raising the stakes in new dialogic encounters. *Journal of Early Childhood Research*, 11 (1), 78–92.

Harwood, D., Klopper, A., Osanyin, A. & Vanderlee, M. (2013). 'It's more than care': Early childhood educators' concepts of professionalism. *Early Years: An International Research Journal*, 33 (1), 4–17.

Hochschild, A. (2002) Emotional labour. In S. Jackson & S. Scott (eds), *Gender: A Sociological Reader* (pp. 192–196). London: Routledge. (Original work published 1983).

Hymes, J.L. (1946) The war babies are coming to school. *Educational Leadership*, 4 (3), 188–192.

John, K. (2008) Sustaining the leaders of children's centres: The role of leadership mentoring. *European Early Childhood Education Research Journal*, 16(1), 53–66.

Layen, S. (2015) Do reflections on personal autobiography as captured in narrated life-stories illuminate leadership development in the field of early childhood? *Professional Development in Education*, 41 (2), 273–289.

Lebedeva, G. (2015) Building brains one relationship at a time. *Exchange*, 11, Nov/Dec 2015, 21–25.

Lynch, K., Baker, J. & Lyons, M. (2009) *Affective Equality: Love, Care and Injustice.* Basingstoke: Palgrave Macmillan.

Manning-Morton, J. (2006) The personal is professional: Professionalism and the birth to threes practitioner. *Contemporary Issues in Early Childhood*, 7 (1), 42–52.

Mathers, S., Eisenstadt, N., Sylva, K., Soukakou, E. & Ereky-Stevens, K. (2014) *Sound Foundations: A Review of the Research Evidence on Quality of Early Childhood Education and Care for Children Under Three.* Oxford: Oxford University and The Sutton Trust.

Matthews, P., Rea, S., Hill, R. & Gu, Q. (2014) Freedom to lead: A study of outstanding primary school leadership in England. Online at: https://www.gov.uk/government/publications

Mitchell, J., Riley, P. & Loughran, J. (2010) Leading professional learning in schools: Emotion in action. *Teacher Development*, 14 (4), 533–547.

Noddings, N. (2001) The care tradition: Beyond "add women and stir". *Theory into Practice*, 40 (1), 29–34.

Noddings, N. (2007) *Philosophy of Education*, 2nd edition. Cambridge, MA, USA: Westview Press.

Nutbrown, C. (2013) *Foundations for Quality: The Independent Review of Early Education and Childcare Qualifications (The Nutbrown Report)*. London: Department for Education.

Osgood, J. (2011) Contested constructions of professionalism within the nursery. In L. Miller & C. Cable (eds), *Professionalization, Leadership and Management in the Early Years* (pp. 107–118). London: Sage Publications.

Owen, P.M. & Gillentine, J. (2011) Please touch the children: Appropriate touch in the primary classroom. *Early Child Development and Care*, 181 (6), 857–868.

Page, J. & Elfer, P. (2013) The emotional complexity of attachment interactions in nursery. *European Early Childhood Education Research Journal*, 21 (4), 553–567.

Piper, H. & Smith, H. (2003) 'Touch' in educational and child care settings: Dilemmas and responses. *British Educational Research Journal*, 29 (6), 879–894.

Powell, S. & Goouch, K. (2012) Whose hand rocks the cradle? Parallel discourses in the baby room. *Early Years*, 32 (2), 113–127.

Rose, J. (2009) *Independent Review of the Primary Curriculum: Final Report*. Nottingham: Department of Schools Children and Families.

Sikes, P. & Piper, H. (2010) *Researching Sex and Lies in the Classroom: Allegations of Sexual Misconduct in Schools*. Abingdon: Routledge.

Conclusion

Complex and joyful work with individual children

We began this book by stating that childhood is a special time to enjoy. It is also a time of rapid development, as young children are wonderful and unique human beings with a propensity to learn and develop at a breath-taking pace and in unexpected ways. With appropriate support from peers, familiar adults and communities, children can develop positive identities, good self-esteem and the confidence to express their opinions in a range of contexts. They can demonstrate affection, care and concern for those around them and work effectively with others to achieve goals and aspirations. The great mystery is how young children manage to do all these things. There is no one single answer to this question as children are unique individuals, with different personalities and diverse backgrounds and experiences. Children come from a range of social, economic and cultural backgrounds, have different priorities within their families, and live in very varied homes and communities. So young children's learning is complex and there is no one single technique or programme that is a 'one size fits all' tool for success. Published toolkits do not easily match children's complex emotional, social and sensory learning trajectories. Therefore, adults and professionals who work and interact with young children have a momentous responsibility in the work they do. It is a great privilege to be involved in young children's lives and help them with their learning.

People to do this complex work

What sorts of people are needed to carry out this momentous and complex work in non-familial, professional settings? People with a passion for working with children. So much of the role of educating and caring for very young children is done in a natural way. People draw on their own experiences of being loved and cared for, as well as their own experiences of loving and caring for others in their family and community contexts. At the same time, however, and as we have argued in this book, it is important to have extensive knowledge about how children learn and develop emotionally, through their senses and socially in order to do the work well. Such learning, whether it be gained through programmes of study in further or higher education, apprenticeship programmes, or from experience of working in different contexts, enriches the work these professionals do. Structured learning allows practitioners to draw on different models of practice, relate what they do to different theories, reflect on their own practice, understand the value of learning about different ways of doing things, and be able to explain to others, including parents and professionals, why they adopt a particular approach with a particular child.

Crucially, people who do this work enter into relationships with individual children and their families. They attend to the children in their care with genuine interest and affection. They communicate well with children and their families, want the best for them, and think deeply about their learning and development. People who work with very young children are likely to be highly qualified, or want to aspire to learn more at all times. They are lifelong learners, with a desire to support young children to develop well, be happy, resilient, confident and self-aware. These experts know how to support children in different ways, by stimulating their senses, recognising the learning that can happen in different social contexts, and by attending to their emotional well-being.

This is complex work, in a richly diverse world with different beliefs about best practice in childcare and education. Professionals in early childhood contexts, therefore, are special people with a vocation for the work they do. They love their work, and they love the children they are responsible for. They form good relationships with the people they work with and the families and communities they serve. These admirable people are lifelong learners, with an unstoppable hunger for more knowledge and understanding about their work.

Hopes and aspirations

At the beginning of the book we talked about the importance of early experiences in life. We emphasised the important role of adults as they contribute to children's happiness and help them to communicate well with others. We considered different sets of international principles and put forward our own. We said that childhood is a special time to enjoy. Children learn about the world through their emotions, their senses and the people around them. Accordingly, we emphasised the importance for adults to acknowledge children's creations and offer genuine encouragement. Crucially, we said it was important for adults to communicate well with each other and acknowledge when they need more help, for example, from other professionals. Most importantly, we said that highly skilled and emotionally self-aware people were needed for this complex work with babies and very young children.

We end this book with a look to the future. How will we support emotional, sensory and social learning in the early years as we move forward? There will be a need to embrace new technologies. Practitioners will have to be convinced of the value of digital technologies and how these can be used to support children's learning and development. They will need to experience for themselves how digital technologies can support children to be sociable, feel good about their learning, and be motivated to explore their natural environment.

Many children belong to families who have come from far away. Some of their close family members may still live far away. These children bring a wealth of cultural, social and linguistic experiences. Early years practitioners need to tap into this potential, make it their business to know about this diversity and celebrate it. This is something for the children to be proud of. Skilled practitioners need to perceive themselves as global citizens, aware of what is happening in different parts of the world as it relates to the lives of the children they care for.

Early years leaders need to establish environments in which their teams can talk freely about the issues they face in their daily work. Nurseries and settings need to be fear-free, safe places where people can articulate concerns, raise questions and feel comfortable that there may be no simple answers or solutions. Early years practitioners are concerned with the individual child. Accordingly, they adapt the curriculum and any prescribed assessments to meet the needs of each child. For example, if a child is newly arrived from a war-torn country or has recently suffered a bereavement, normative expectations will not apply.

It is clear from the above that highly sensitive, experienced and knowledgeable people are needed for this wonderful work. This is no light or easy career path, but one to be proud of, to reflect upon and to build on throughout life. Early years practitioners embrace change. Every day with every child is different. They embrace new technologies and diverse socio-cultural heritages as part of their everyday work. These knowledgeable and skilled people engage with research, both as researcher-practitioners and as research-informed professionals. They are hungry for new knowledge and ready to try out new approaches to support children to develop as happy, sociable and confident human beings. Early years practitioners have the awesome responsibility of nurturing the people of tomorrow.

Index